THE GIRL FROM RIGA

A memoir

Sibilla Hershey

ISBN: 1544196105
ISBN 13: 9781544196107
Library of Congress Control Number: 2017904310
CreateSpace Independent Publishing Platform
North Charleston, South Carolina
Cover Art by Henry White, Petaluma, CA

ACKNOWLEDGMENTS

Essential editorial and technical support was provided by Mike Alber of Midnight Writers Productions, Santa Rosa, California; John Dale Hershey, Portland, Oregon and John W. B. Hershey, Berkeley, California.

This book is dedicated to my parents Viktors and Karola Dale, my brother, Kornelijs (Neil) Dale and to my husband Gerald Gibbons.

INTRODUCTION

This book has curious beginnings. During World War II, my brother and I spent four summers on our maternal grandmother's farm on the outskirts of Riga, Latvia. I was between five and eight years old, and my brother was two years older than me. On the farm we experienced the wonders of the outdoor world with all our senses, listening to the sounds of summer: the hum of insects, the crowing of roosters, the singing of the cuckoo and the nightingale. We inhaled summer scents: pine sap, the elixir of turpentine, the smell of cow manure, the ozone of the air after a thunderstorm. We collected mushrooms and ate wild berries in the nearby birch forest. We collected wildflowers and picked worms off cabbages. This was a place full of wonder because the world was still new to us. It was also full of horror because World War II was raging around us.

We lived in a combat zone without being conscious of it since such experience was the norm to us. We watched planes take off from the nearby airport to intercept the opposing aircraft and fight the war in the air above us. Troops walked through our land, requesting food. At one time we saw the city of Riga, where we were born, burning on the horizon like a stage set. During those years, part of the time we were under Russian occupation, then later under German. We heard of deportations and executions. People disappeared. This world fascinated me so much that when I learned that books existed, I thought that someday someone should write one about these experiences.

In the summer of 1944, as the war intensified, we had to flee Soviet troops, who were invading Latvia once more. We became refugees and lived in refugee camps. We had to learn new languages. Six years after the war ended, we came to the United States. By the time I graduated from high school in Brooklyn, New York, I had attended school for only ten years in three different languages: Latvian, German, and English.

There was no time to write a book about what I lived through as a child when I came to America. As war refugees who had fled with only the clothes on our backs and what we could carry, our family needed to survive economically. Instead of writing, I concentrated on numbers and symbols and earned a degree in chemistry. For several years I worked as a medical research technician at a lab bench. Then I married and became a mom and later went back to school to study social work because inside I was injured I wanted to learn how to help those who were wounded by life because I myself desperately needed such help.

Late in life, after taking a poetry class, I started to write. I found kindred spirits in the Sacramento, California, literary community and had poems published locally. I joined writing groups. I wrote autobiographical poetry. I felt compelled to tell my story. My brother, Neil, did too. He also started to write about our shared childhood experiences during World War II, especially about the time we spent on our grandmother's farm on the outskirts of Riga, the capitol of Latvia.

Neil and I lived in different States and shared our stories by email. At some point we decided to prepare a manuscript that contained both his and my wartime stories. However, my brother died before this project could be implemented. I have incorporated some of his writing in this book.

After I retired from working for the State of California, I attended a memoir-writing group, where we responded to prompts such as "My first home..." Then I decided to write what I wanted to write, not just about topics suggested by a teacher. I started to write a memoir, stopped writing, started, and stopped again.

Finally I looked for an editor. I found one by going to Google. Google directed me to Thumbtack. The names of three editors came up on my computer screen. I interviewed a young man named Mike. I only met him once, but there was something about him that made me want to share my story with him. I gave him a packet of loosely put-together pages of a memoir written during different periods of my life. "Throw out anything that does not belong there," I told him.

Since we lived about seventy-five miles apart, the editing was done by e-mail. I was enjoying this exchange so much that I kept writing additional material. I did not want this fun to end. Like a modern-day Scheherazade I kept e-mailing stories to him. Some were stories that I had written a long time ago, while others were recent recollections of a distant past. He did not keep all of them, but he learned a great deal about me through this process. It helped him understand me as a person. This knowledge came through in his edits. Sometimes he rephrased my thoughts and feelings better than I could do myself. Eventually that fun had to end. Here is my story.

PROLOGUE

On an isolated farm, not far from the Baltic Sea, two children were playing in the deep grass by an irrigation ditch. The ground was damp. Their grandmother had warned them not to sit on the ground before the first thunderstorm of the summer. She had warned of serious consequences: illnesses of bones, joints, and kidneys.

They had broken the rule and lay stretched out on the ground watching the sky. A hawk circled above them. The girl, who was more influenced by predictions of mysterious illnesses than her brother, sat up first. She picked a stalk of grass with a plume of reddish blooms, ran her fingers up the stem until the cluster of flowers appeared between her thumb and forefinger.

"A hen," she exclaimed.

The boy picked another stalk and repeated the motion. "A rooster," he declared. His cluster was higher than hers and had a tall spike of crushed blooms.

Clouds thickened and grew large on the horizon. The girl thought she heard a distant thunderclap.

"No, that was an explosion, a bomb," the boy said. An airplane had passed overhead earlier. He suggested that they hide in the haystack in the event a bomb was dropped. The hay would protect them from the shrapnel.

Instead of heading toward the haystack they walked back to the farmhouse, where their grandmother had been making raspberry jam over the wood stove in the kitchen. Earlier they had watched her stir down the pink foam. They were hungry. As they got closer, they saw chickens running around the courtyard, screeching. A hawk had dug its claws into the neck of a chicken. Grandmother was thrashing at the hawk with a broomstick. When she saw the children, she berated them for not keeping watch over the chickens. She told them that from now on they would have to stay in the courtyard and guard the chickens. They had lost their freedom to roam.

THE GIRL FROM RIGA

On a sunny Sunday afternoon in Riga, Latvia, our family of four was on the way to a park. My father, mother, brother, and I were crossing a broad boulevard. I was about four or five years old; my brother was six or seven. Both my brother and I were holding on to each of my father's hands when my mother said in a sad voice, "Doesn't anybody want to hold my hand?" I dropped my father's hand and took hers. I felt sorry for her and felt it my duty to hold her hand, but my heart belonged to Daddy.

My father was the nurturing parent in the family. As a small child I used to stand at the window to catch a glimpse of my father on his way home from work. When he arrived, my brother and I rushed toward him. Sometimes he gave us a lift, sometimes a spin. He read fairy tales to us at bedtime.

There was no need to stand at the window to watch for my mother. I could hear her purposeful footsteps a block away. I listened to the click-click of her heels as she entered the foyer and then again as she climbed the three flights of stairs. As she entered the apartment, her footsteps receded. She went straight to an activity such as making a phone call, giving orders to the cook, or lighting a cigarette. She possessed a restless, elusive energy that both fascinated and disturbed me. She was always searching for something, and nothing could distract her from her pursuit. I remember her frequent searches for her cuticle scissors. "Where are my little scissors? Have you seen my little scissors? Did you take my scissors? Where did you put them?" I often joined in the search just to end the turmoil that her search caused in me. At other times she would search for the right words for her next poems, and at other times, after a drink or two, she would delve into the meaning of life. When the meaning eluded her, she wept, "Life has no meaning. Life has no meaning."

My mother was short, with almost black hair and blue eyes. She possessed a restless energy and flamboyance that, when I was a young child, I coveted.

Early in life I wanted to be like her. Like my father, she was a lawyer. My father worked for the Latvian government, in the Ministry of Finance; my mother worked for an organization similar to the American Legal Aid Society, providing law services to the poor.

A few years later, we learned the details of the event that had impacted our mother's life deeply. Her father had been murdered when she was fourteen years old. At the time of the murder, she had lived on a farm with my grandparents in the outskirts of Riga. Our maternal grandmother, Sofija, still lived there.

THE FAMILY

The persons who impacted my early years were my parents, my brother, a strict nanny named Frau Weiss, and my maternal grandmother. There had been another, younger nanny during the first two years of my life, and it may have been she who had pulled me through the warm water of the Baltic Sea with such joy.

Frau Weiss was a forerunner of the dictatorial regimes that would soon engulf our country and our family in the figures of Stalin and Hitler. Frau Weiss was of Baltic German origin. She was elderly, stout, and fluent in Latvian, German, and Russian. She was hired to teach my brother and me these languages.

If she did not succeed much on the linguistic front, she made great strides instilling terror in us.

I remember having fun with my brother enacting a scene from a story that we had heard from a nurse while we had been hospitalized with scarlet fever. This was during my third summer. Upon discharge from the hospital we had been sent to stay at the summer cottage at the seashore, where Frau Weiss ruled unsupervised during the week while my parents worked in the city. One afternoon my brother and I were on the lawn trying to climb some bushes, laughing loudly and reciting the rhyme we had learned at the hospital from a nurse, when Frau Weiss appeared on the porch wearing dark sunglasses. Because we could not see her eyes, we assumed that she could not see us, so we continued our game. Suddenly, Frau Weiss pounced on us and dragged us back into the house to stand facing the wall, each in a separate corner.

Frau Weiss had Sundays off. It was a joy to walk with my father on Sunday mornings on sandy paths through pine forests, my father still wearing his striped pajamas, while my mother slept in late at the summer cottage. On some Sundays, while Mama slept, Papa read us fairy tales or taught us how to play board games. He taught us how to play chess, checkers, and Parcheesi. In the evening he read us bedtime stories from illustrated books. He was fond of relating adventure and disaster stories, such as telling us about the San Francisco earthquake and the sinking of the *Titanic*.

I remember standing at the window of my father's study waiting for him to come home from the office one winter evening. It was growing dark outside. While I waited, I passed the time counting the lights going on in the city. A light snow was falling on the already snowy streets. Suddenly, my father stood in the doorway. He walked over to his desk and switched on the light: "Let there be light." The green lamp cast a circle of light. I rushed over to him. He picked me up and carried me over to the globe for my lesson in geography. There were snowflakes on the shoulders of his black overcoat and he smelled of wet wool.

Our father was born into a Latvian family, under luckier stars than our mother, on a farm near the Baltic Sea when Latvia was still a province of the Russian Empire, in 1888. According to church records, the Dahle family has lived in that region for several hundred years, since about 1760. His father was a customs official at the Port of Riga. The Dahle family came originally from Ikskile, a Swedish settlement on the river Daugava, and were farmers. He was one of seven children, five of whom survived into adulthood. He was the second oldest of the surviving children. He attended grade school and high school in Riga, following the classical education model. He studied both Greek and Latin, and when we were children he would quote all sorts of Latin phrases to us, such as "Sic transit gloria mundi."

My father was forty-four years old when he married my mother, who was twenty-six. By the time I came along, when he was forty-eight, he had already lived the greater part of his life, a life rich in drama and historic events. He had studied law at the University of Moscow and attended artillery school in St. Petersburg. He fought in the Russian military in Turkey during World War I. When the Russian Empire crumbled during the Bolshevik Revolution in 1917, he returned to the land of his birth and fought for Latvian independence. Latvia emerged as an independent Baltic state, along with Estonia and Lithuania, in 1918.

Outwardly traditional, even stuffy looking, my father harbored tastes for exotic women and expensive furniture, a love for the bottle and an even stronger love for his children. During the years of Latvian independence, when he practiced law, my father would go on solo riding vacations in Hungary where, the story goes, he pursued gypsy women. There may be some truth to this. I remember the ornate Hungarian doll that he brought back for me from one of his trips. She was dressed in a beautiful red Hungarian folk costume that was not removable.

She sat on the back of the couch, out of reach and unavailable for play.

In 1932, my father married Karola Auzaraja, who was also a lawyer and a poet. It was his second marriage, and her third. Two children resulted from this marriage. My brother Kornelijs, later known as Neil, was born in 1933, and I followed in 1935. Our mother was seventeen years younger than our father. We remember a balding man with graying hair, even when we were little, but we remember seeing photos of him when he was younger with light-brown, wavy hair.

My brother wrote about a photo of my father taken late in my father's life, and the differences between father and son:

> This photo shows a spiffily dressed older gentleman leaning against the bridge railing and smoking a cigarette. He is wearing a hat, a suit with a tie, and an overcoat. The overcoat is open and he has his right hand in the coat pocket of the suit, while his left hand holds the cigarette. In the background one can see a pond, trees and some shrubbery and further back some apartment buildings. The location is the Japanese Garden section of the Brooklyn Botanical Gardens. The time

is sometime in the late nineteen fifties. It is a black and white photo. I do not know who took the photo, but it is quite likely that I did. The gentleman in the photo is my father. This photo [was] taken late in his life.

He was quite different from me. He liked to dress well, while I could claim to have invented "grunge" some fifty plus years ago… He observed all the social niceties. He was quite proper, [which is] definitely not true of me. He was quite orderly, while I am an advocate of cluttered desks and horizontal filing systems. Are my mother's genetic traits predominant in me? He was my father[;] there certainly must be something of him in me.

Short, dark, and flamboyant, my mother was a descendant of the Livs, who in Latvian were known as *Libiesi*. The Livs are a small ethnic minority in Latvia who are now almost extinct. The Liv language resembles Estonian and Finnish more than Latvian. The Livs are generally shorter and darker than most Latvians and have higher cheekbones. My maternal cousin Andris, the one who believes that our family is cursed, looks like he could be a descendant of Genghis Khan himself. The Mongolian hordes did penetrate the region that is now Latvia, at one time in history.

Due to her father's violent death, my mother chose her own path early in life. A year after his murder, at the age of fifteen and against her mother's wishes, she left the family farm and went to work in Riga, at a legal firm owned her uncle who was an attorney. While working as a typist, she met her first husband, named Von Leitendorf, an attorney and a descendant of Baltic German nobility. He was a distant relative by marriage, and was twenty-seven years her senior. This marriage produced no children. A few years into this marriage my mother fell in love with another Baltic German this one a few years her junior, named Von Schwanenbach, who at that time was a tenant in the Von Leitendorf household. Von Schwanenbach, a dance teacher, turned out to prefer men to women. This marriage also ended after a few years, and again there were no children.

My mother studied law at the newly established University of Latvia in Riga. She also started to write poetry. This interest brought her together with my father's sister Austra, who also wrote poetry. Austra had married a divorced man. My father's family had disapproved of the marriage, and none of my father's five brothers nor either parent had attended the wedding. The only family member to attend was my father, who was loyal to his only sister.

My parents did not meet at that wedding but a number of years later, after my father had also become a divorced man. His first wife, Vera, the daughter of a wealthy restaurant owner, ran off with a charismatic matinee idol and fortune-teller named the Sphinx. There were no children from my father's first marriage.

One October, on All Souls' Day, my father took me to visit his parents' graves in Riga. It was a chilly, overcast day. Brown leaves covered the gravel paths that separated the rows of graves. It was my first visit to a cemetery. My father stopped in front of a grave that had a granite headstone and was surrounded by an iron chain. He placed some chrysanthemums on the mound and then stood silently, with his head bowed and hands folded. There was a smell of decay in the air. I was convinced it came from the dead. I kept holding my breath in order to prevent the dead from invading me.

In the family album there is a photo of the people who attended my father's fiftieth birthday party, about thirty in number, all close friends and relatives. The photo was taken in my parents' apartment in Riga on March 10, 1938. At the gathering are two Latvian cabinet ministers, one being the Minister of Education, Atis Kenins, who married my father's sister. They lived in the apartment directly below us. At the very center of the last row, standing behind my seated parents and grandmother, is the barely thirty-year-old maverick Minister of Finance, whose vitality and charisma were apparent even to me as a child. My brother and I do not appear in the picture because we were already asleep in the nursery when the party took place.

The destructive forces of the Second World War would tear this group apart and scatter its members to the four corners of the earth. Caught between Stalin and Hitler, in less than six years most of the people gathered here would lose their professions, possessions, incomes, homes, families, and country. All the men present had built their careers on their verbal skills. They were lawyers, writers, and politicians. None of them had any technical, transferable skills. Few would be able to earn a living abroad without doing manual labor, and they would never prosper again economically.

My father's brother Modris, who was a member of the Latvian National Guard, and his family were deported east to Siberia. Their family would be among the more than fifteen thousand Latvians deported to Stalin's slave-labor camps. They would spend eighteen years there before returning to Latvia, his daughters' spirits broken and his son's character shaped by Siberian winters.

The Russians deported Austra, and her husband, Atis, south to Kazakhstan. A family friend who was at the party, Karlis Skalbe, a nationally known poet and writer of children's stories, fled north to Sweden, where he died shortly after the war. He had predicted his demise in a foreign land in a poem that he had written during the war.

My parents fled west to Germany and later to the United States. We would spend six years in displaced persons camps in Germany before four hundred thousand refugees would be admitted to the United States under the Displaced Persons Act.

My father's brother Pauls Dale, a professor of philosophy and psychology and whose daughter had tuberculosis of the bone and could not travel, remained in Latvia. They survived under Communism with the help of a former neighbor, who had become the leader of the Latvian Communist Party. My grandmother remained alone on her farm and outlived my mother by several years.

My brother, Neil, beat me in the race to enter this world by almost two years, and he picked a good day for his arrival: November 11. Since he was born on Armistice Day, there was always a parade on his birthday.

Before the war my parents rented summer homes on the Baltic, a different one each year. I remember at least two residences. They correspond to my third and fourth summers. The memories are sketchy, discontinuous, and not necessarily consecutive. These prewar memories are tinted with a golden aura, like happy dreams that brighten the mood even after their contents have faded.

I remember being pulled through water by a woman who was not my mother. We were in the sea, going up and down on huge swells. The woman was laughing, calling out to me, "You're swimming." I had no fear of the water. The temperature was just right. I still remember the delicious feeling of weightlessness and effortless motion. The woman who pulled me through the water may have been my first nanny, who was replaced by Frau Weiss when I was about three or four years old.

My mother told me she was in the garden of one of those rented summer homes by the sea when her labor began. My birth progressed faster than expected, and she had to be rushed to the hospital because I had the umbilical cord around my neck. I was born in the early evening of July 19, 1935, at the Second City Hospital in a suburb of Riga.

Since he was with me throughout my childhood, it is hard to pinpoint my earliest memory of my brother. What stands out is a long, gray winter afternoon in Riga. We were alone in the nursery playing quietly, each with our own toys, on a wooden parquet floor. Everything was very still. I missed the hustle and bustle of the usual household activities and the attention of others but I was still too young to express myself, so I simply said out loud, "I want more noise." Immediately Neil started to pound his fists on the floor. This was not what I had in mind, but I was surprised and touched by his wish to please me. This is my first conscious memory of my lifelong love for my brother. In fact, I credit my brother with the development of a whole range of emotions in me.

One summer afternoon, when Neil and I were still spending the summers at the seashore, we were playing in a sandbox in the back of our parents' summer cottage on the Baltic. There were two other boys my brother's age in the sandbox with us. I was happily arranging my doll tea service on a wooden ledge and turning out sand cakes. Suddenly, there was my brother peeing into my teacup. Then the two other boys joined him. Outraged, I started to cry and turned and ran back to the house to report the injustice to Frau Weiss. On the way, blinded by tears, I fell into a bucket of water that Frau Weiss had placed on the lawn to catch rainwater. She used the rainwater for washing her hair. Bewildered, I caught the hem of my skirt and ran into the house, carrying rainwater gathered in my skirt, not knowing what to do with it. By then I was sobbing so hard that I couldn't relate the outrage to the adults in the house. Frau Weiss may have felt a bit guilty for leaving the bucket in the middle of the lawn. She held a cold spoon against the bump on my head but failed to scold my brother. Later, Neil even had the gall to laugh at me for bringing a lapful of water into the house. I still have a scar above my right eyebrow from hitting the rim of that metal bucket.

I did get the upper hand at least once. Early on a Saturday morning, while our parents were still sleeping, Frau Weiss, Neil, and I walked to a kiosk to buy a newspaper. It was a quiet morning in a small seaside town with very few people about and no traffic in the streets. Frau Weiss stopped across the street from the kiosk. She gave Neil some money and asked him to run across and buy the morning paper. He crossed the street but then turned around, looked back at us, and started to whimper. "Frau Weiss, I can't see you," he said.

She called him back and gave the money to me. This was my moment. I looked at the street and saw no immediate danger. I dashed across the street, gave the money to the vendor, and returned victorious with the newspaper. Later I felt smug and pleased when Frau Weiss related this event to our parents.

I remember the late-summer afternoon when I first learned about the war, even though I was only five years old. I was alone in the garden of a rented summer home, slowly touching the velvety blooms of pansies and marigolds, rubbing them between my fingers for texture and scent. Time passed slowly. It grew dark. I had an odd sensation of something not being quite right. Why had those in charge of my daily routines forgotten to call me in for supper? I wandered toward the house. Inside, the lights were on, and from the kitchen entrance I could see the shapes of the adults huddled around the dining-room table. No one took notice of me as I entered the room. Later it was explained to me that the war had started, but I had no concept of war. I only remember the sense of gloom that settled on everything like stale air.

SOFIJA

She first appeared in my life, all dressed in black, when I was about three years old and she was in her early sixties. She sat in a chair facing us in the nursery that I shared with my brother at our city home in Riga and sang a sorrowful song in a high-pitched voice. Her voice provoked a sweet pain in me, a sorrow that frightened me.

I did not know how to tell her to stop, so I said, "I don't like your singing."

She stopped abruptly. "You don't like my singing?" she asked, sounding hurt. I felt guilty and a little angry for initiating this unpleasantness.

Sofija was my mother's mother. Widowed, she lived on a farm on the outskirts of Riga. She walked with a permanent limp that, my mother explained, she got from falling when she got off a still-moving streetcar.

According to my mother, Sofija had had an exceptional voice when she was young and had been encouraged in her youth to develop her voice professionally. However, she refused to step on the stage because she thought it was unbecoming for a woman. She was courted by a local farmer but refused to marry him because he had prominent varicose veins. At age twenty-five she married her first cousin, Karlis, also a farmer. In 1905, at age thirty, she gave birth to her only child, Karola, who thirty years later became my mother.

I only knew Sofija in her old age, after she had survived a mass murder on the farm on August 9, 1919, that took the lives of her husband, a niece, and a nephew. She had lived through the bloodbath in the dark of the night and stood the killer down. At the time of the murder my mother was fourteen years old. In May 1941, when my brother and I started to spend summers on the farm, we were not yet aware of the dark history of the place.

THE FARM

When World War II started we no longer spent summers at cottages near the seashore. My father lost his job as a judge and was at risk of being deported to Siberia, which was a common Communist practice for punishing the nationalistic and educated people of an occupied country. My father's sister's husband, who lived a floor below us in the family apartment house in Riga, was deported to Siberia. My father escaped deportation by riding the streetcar at night or hiding in the woods near our grandmother's farm. One half of our six-room apartment was confiscated. The apartment had two entrances, one leading to our living area and the other to my father's study, and two other rooms. Strangers were settled in the part that contained my father's study.

Starting in the summer of 1941, my brother and I spent the next four summers on our maternal grandmother's farm. After the war started, Frau Weiss had returned to her hometown of Pozen, in German-occupied Poland, and Grandma became the ultimate authority in our lives.

On our first evening on the farm, in early May 1941, Sofija appeared on the kitchen doorstep and called my brother and me in for supper. We ate boiled potatoes, salted herring, and a few leaves of lettuce dressed with a dab of sour cream. We would eat a similar meal each evening for the rest of the summer. When dinner was done, she cleared the table and washed the dishes. Then she lit an oil lamp, since the farm had no electricity, and sang sorrowful songs as the light grew dim. I no longer objected to her singing. When dark descended on the farm, she sent my brother and me to bed.

During the four summers that my brother and I spent at Sofija's farm both Russian and German troops moved through our land. On summer days Neil and I would lie on our backs in the meadow and watch German Messerschmitts and Russian MiGs engage in warfare above us. Sometimes a plane caught on fire and went down in flames. We saw men parachute from aircraft and watched the breeze carry their chutes toward the ground like dandelion seeds. They disappeared in the forest. Later some of these men appeared at our doorstep and begged for food. Only one woman knew how to appease the strangers at the door and protect us from harm.

The farm was an isolated place set in low-lying meadows on the Baltic coast, next to a white birch forest. In the spring the meadows would flood. The floods brought fields of yellow buttercups. Summer arrived with white daisies, blue dragonflies, cicadas, fireflies, and other insects that would hum and buzz until the hay was made. It was here that I first experienced the wonder of my uniqueness in the universe, a sense of self that felt both marvelous and immortal.

My first memory of the farm is like a distant dream. My brother and I were outside in a meadow that bordered the farmhouse. The meadow was full of little blue flowers. It was twilight and quite chilly. I was shivering. Neil was picking the flowers. It was May 19, 1941. I remember the date well because the next day, May 20, was my name day. I knew that he would present the little bouquet to me as a name-day gift the next day, and I was a little disappointed that he was not going to give me a more exciting present.

The farmhouse was fairly close to Riga. We could see the Riga airport well enough to see planes land and take off. Behind the airport we could see the taller structures of Riga. At that time the tallest structures of downtown Riga were church spires.

The farm consisted of two buildings, the house and a barn. The barn was for the livestock, which consisted of two cows and some chickens. Above the barn was a loft, where hay was stored. The farm was a primitive place with no electricity, no running water, and a drop toilet. Next to the farmhouse was a birch forest where my brother and I picked berries and mushrooms. On the other side of the forest were sand dunes with scrub pines, and beyond the dunes was the river Bullupe. There were no roads nearby, only sandy trails for hay wagons and cows. At day's end my brother and I washed our bodies in an irrigation ditch. The usual supper consisted of boiled potatoes seasoned with dill, yogurt, and a salad dressed with sour cream. At sundown Grandma lit an oil lamp and entertained us by singing sad tunes like the ones she sang for me when I first met her. I grew fond of her sorrowful voice. We went to bed when it got dark and got up at sunrise to spend another day in the fields and meadows. The war seemed far, far away.

My brother and I roamed through the fields and the forest, picking wild berries, scattering cow dung, and plucking worms off cabbages, chores assigned to us by Grandma. One of our assigned tasks was also to protect the chickens from hawks. Once we wandered through the forest into the dunes, and we enjoyed the thrill of rolling down them. When we got back to the farm, the chickens were in an uproar and so was Grandma. A hawk had carried off one of the chickens.

My brother omitted Frau Weiss from his memoir and declared our Grandma the ultimate authority of our early childhood years. He writes:

> My sister, two years my junior, and I had only one grandparent, our maternal grandmother. Most people have more than one grandparent, but our grandparents on our father's side both had died the year before I was born, and my maternal grandfather was murdered in 1919. My earliest memories of my grandmother are from times she visited us in our apartment in Riga. We looked forward to her visits; it is possible that she brought us some small gifts, or some candy or fruit. She seemed to project a sense of benevolence. Grandmother did not live in the city[;] she lived on her farm, but not too far from Riga.
>
> Her name was Sofija and she was born on May 15, 1875. I do not know how she and her husband acquired this farm near Riga, because she was born near another[,] smaller city[,] named Saldus, which was a considerable

distance from Riga. Her husband was named Karlis[,] and[,] according to my sister, he was her first cousin. People talk about skeletons in the closet. Maybe this is one of ours. They had one child, my mother, who was born in 1905.

According to my brother's knowledge of World War II history, the Soviets demanded the right to establish military bases in the Baltic countries and Finland in 1939. The Baltic countries acceded to this demand, and the result was their occupation by the Soviets in 1940. Finland declined, leading to the Russo-Finnish War, which cost many Finnish lives, and even more Russian ones. This war preserved the independence of Finland. So in 1941 Latvia was a Soviet Socialist Republic, while Finland remained an independent country. My father, considered an unreliable nationalist by Soviet standards, lost his job, and our parents felt that the farm would be the safest place for us children. Thus, in the summer of 1941 Grandma became the ultimate authority in our lives.

Later that winter I watched the Russian troops march through Riga. The soldiers wore moss-colored felt boots. My own boots were made of leather and I felt an odd pity for the soldiers. A picture of a Russian general named Voroshilov appeared in the window of the photographer's shop that was located on the ground floor of the apartment house where we lived in Riga. He seemed very handsome to me in his uniform—my first infatuation with a military man.

My brother remembers the farm as a workplace:

My memories of the next four summers are somewhat sketchy, but I clearly remember that Grandmother did not believe in idleness. My sister and I had various duties assigned [to us], mostly to do with gardening, such as weeding, picking off green worms from the cabbage plants, picking wild berries and mushrooms in the nearby forest, and bringing home dry branches from the woods that were used as kindling for the wood stove in the kitchen. The job I disliked the most was weeding. In effect my grandmother is responsible for my dislike of gardening in adult life. I did enjoy the berry and mushroom picking in the forest very much, and therefore should give credit to my grandma for my enthusiasm [for] outdoor pursuits in later life.

The farm provided much of the food we ate. We had a cow that gave milk. And Grandmother insisted that we each drink a liter of milk a day. Then hens laid eggs and all sorts of vegetables came from the garden[;]

plus there were berries—raspberries and currants, both red and black. After the first summer we also had a hive of bees—thus some honey. From sugar beets molasses [was] made, [which we] used in lieu of sugar, which was difficult to get in wartime.

The summers I spent on Grandmother's farm seemed to be the best times of my childhood. There was enough free time, and on weekends usually our parents would come. I don't recall ever being bored.

All in all, I think my grandmother had a pretty rough life, losing her husband, living through two wars, running the farm by herself, and dealing with two grandchildren, who were not exactly exemplary and well-behaved children, for four summers when she was already in her sixties. It could not have been easy.

Cooking on the farm was done on a wood-fired stove. Water came from a pump in the kitchen. There was also a well on the property, which was not used due to the convenience of the kitchen pump. The toilet, a gravity type, was on the primitive side, and as it was indoors, chemicals were dumped to minimize the stink. The farm was not connected to electricity until 1942. In a northern country like Latvia summer days were pretty long, and thus not much kerosene was used in the summer.

Since my brother was older by two years, he was more aware of the sequence of the military actions taking place in Latvia at the beginning of the war. Here are his recollections:

World War II was happening while we spent the summers on the farm. In 1940 the Soviet Union occupied the Baltic Countries. On June 22, 1941, Germany attacked the Soviet Union. We saw German planes bombing the Riga airport in late June. On June 30, 1941, we saw fires burning in Riga that were set by the retreating Soviet Army. On July 1 the Germans entered Riga. Our mother, who was then in the city, witnessed that. Our father was on the farm. He appeared a few days earlier out of the forest[,] where he had been hiding out to avoid deportation by the Soviets.

In the summer of 1944 we saw the Russians bombing Riga at night[;] we heard the antiaircraft batteries firing and saw the explosions in the night sky. The Russians tried to bomb the bridges over the river Daugava, but did not hit any.

THE MURDER

The farm was the place where my brother and I
developed our lifelong love for outdoor life. It
was also the place where our maternal grandfather
was murdered. I don't remember when I first heard
of the murder. The story came to me in bits and pieces from my mother on the rare visits she made to the
farm during the four summers that my brother and I
spent there during the war, when I was between ages
five and nine. She spoke of it in a pensive voice, more
to herself than to me, as if still weighing the mat-
ter. "My father always carried a gun. He slept with
a gun." She talked tentatively, as if still wondering

how this could have happened when he was so well armed.

According to my mother's account, two of my mother's cousins had also been killed on the same night as my grandfather. My mother said, "The male cousin, eighteen, was as strong as an ox. He could have overcome the killer if he had not been attacked in his sleep. He struggled back but he was stabbed too many times. His cries woke us up."

I never brought up the subject of my grandfather's murder and never asked any questions or sought any clarifications. I had learned early not to verbalize my fear. From the fragmented tale that my mother told me over time the following story emerged.

My mother was an only child, but in the summer of 1919, she had company. Three of her cousins, a young man, age eighteen, and two girls, ages seventeen and ten, were staying on the farm.

On the evening of August 8, 1919, my grandfather Karlis, after hauling hay all day, fed and watered his horses and called it quits. My grandmother served the family a supper of potatoes, yogurt, and salted herring. As he ate, my grandfather joked with his wife, daughter, nieces, and nephew. He mentioned that he intended to buy the manor house across the river.

When it grew dark, he led his two horses to a meadow about a quarter of a mile from the house-and-barn complex in the direction of the river. In the meadow he tied the front legs of the horses. Then he settled into a nearby haystack for the night. He had done this many times before, sleeping alongside his horses on pale summer nights, listening to the insects. He studied the constellations as he drifted off to sleep. His universe was shattered later in the night by a blow from an axe, his star extinguished.

After killing my grandfather, the murderer made his way to the farmhouse and entered by the unlocked kitchen door. In a narrow room near the kitchen entrance slept two of my mother's cousins, ages seventeen and eighteen. My mother, then fourteen years old, was ill with the flu. For that reason she slept in a room with her mother, Sofija, and her younger cousin, Billa.

Sometime in the middle of the night my mother, grandmother, and Billa were awakened by the terrified screams of the two older cousins. My grandmother rushed to investigate. In the kitchen she ran into a man that she recognized as a former farmhand. She called him by his name.

The killer hesitated. She talked with him calmly and reasonably, suggesting that instead of killing them he should lock the three of them in a room so he can search the house for any money he believed was hidden there. All this transpired in the dark. There was no electricity at the farm.

The killer locked them in the living room, but in his eagerness to look for money he forgot to secure the shutters of one of the windows. As he frantically searched the house, the three women escaped through the unlocked window. Initially they hid in a field of rye. Then they stumbled through the dark fields to the Indrikson's farm to summon help.

When the rescue party reached the house at dawn, none of the grown-ups were willing to enter. They feared that the murderer might still be inside, waiting. Then my mother, only an adolescent, took charge. She led the rescue party into the house. She told me years later that she had to do that in order to master her terror. At that moment she resolved never to be intimidated by fear again. As long as she lived, my mother always confronted danger with courage and defiance. For me, in a time of war, this became a difficult example to emulate.

Inside they found the dead bodies of the two cousins. The murderer had ransacked the house. Outside there was kindling wood set against the house. The killer had planned to burn the house down with everyone in it. Most likely, he had panicked and fled upon seeing the empty room and the open window.

I heard this story when I was still a child without a fully developed concept of death. It is not surprising that the story I remember differs in detail from my brother's account, which he heard from my grandmother and her brother, Ernest. My brother also recorded the incident in his memoir. According to him, this is what took place on the night of August 8–9, 1919:

The place was my grandmother's farm near Riga, Latvia[;] the time was summer of 1919. World War I had recently ended, but there was still fighting in Latvia, against the Bolsheviks, although at that time the military actions were further east. But it still was a very unsettled time. My maternal grandfather and a friend were some distance from the farmhouse, letting the hobbled horses graze, while they sat at a campfire. My grandfather was napping, and this false friend hit him in the head with a hatchet. The murderer then ran to the farmhouse, where my mother, grandmother[,] and three teenage cousins were staying. The screams of the cousins woke my grandmother and mother, who were in another room. The murderer killed the three teenage cousins but could not break into the room where my mother, age fourteen then[, and her mother were. They had locked and barricaded the door and were able to close the shutters also, and the murderer was not able to hack his way in. They heard him say that he was going to burn down the house. The intruder kept screaming, "Where is the money?" But after some time all the noises had ceased. My grandmother opened the shutters [and] did not see anyone, and she and my mother ran through the fields to the neighbours. Years later we saw where our grandfather was mortally wounded. It was a little hillock some distance from the house. I think that we kids experienced some morbid fascination with all this, but it had happened so long ago that there was nothing scary about it.

Only one photograph of my murdered grandfather has survived, peeled off of some official document, most likely a railroad pass. The photo is of a dark-haired man, about age forty, staring intently into the camera, his hands folded in the lap. His hair is closely cropped. He does not look like a prosperous farmer.

Recently, my brother and I discussed this portion of our shared history in Portland, Oregon. My brother was ill in bed. We argued about the facts until he pointed out that shutters could only be locked from the inside, not the outside. He made a gesture with his arms, imitating the opening and closing of shutters. I had to concede; he had a point.

On rainy days we played on the veranda, a glassed-in porch, where our toy chests were stored. This was the warmest room in the house because of its southern exposure. The windowsills were covered with pieces of dried bread, which our grandmother was saving in anticipation of famine, she told us. Later I found out what the bread was for. Among the dried pieces of bread were several cacti. I remember one of these cacti unfurling a beautiful white blossom on the morning of my birthday.

The farm was only a few miles from the Riga airport, and much of the war was fought above us, in the air. My brother and I watched the action in the sky from the safety of a haystack. Papa had come to the farm to conduct safety drills and to show us how to survive during ground war. He treated us like little soldiers. He said that one of the safest places to be during a war was in the haystack. In a military lecture to us Papa explained, "Strategy calls for the destruction of airports, bridges, harbors, railroads, factories, and cities. The haystack is insignificant and not a target. In the event of an explosion nearby, the haystack will protect you from shrapnel." It was also a comfortable, warm place to sleep during air raids and a good place to hide during active combat, Papa explained. At another time Papa lifted a floorboard in the living room and showed me a gas mask. It looked sinister, like the head of a strange animal, with a snout where the mouth opening was expected to be. Since there was only one gas mask, I wondered who would get to use it and who would be left to die.

My brother and I spent hours on our backs in deep grass watching cloud formations drift by, thunderheads form on the horizon, and planes attack and pursue overhead. We saw plane formations releasing bombs over the airport and learned to distinguish between the sounds of thunder and the sounds of exploding bombs. One day a plane caught on fire. It went down in flames like a giant comet, tracing an arc through the sky, to hit the ground somewhere out of sight. At another times we saw men bail out from an airplane and come down in parachutes, tossed about by currents of air, and land some distance away in a meadow. They disappeared in the forest. Later, men would appear at our grandmother's doorstep and ask for food.

In the fall, we returned to the city. I remember the teacher standing in front of the class on my first day of school in Riga. He was a very handsome young man, with his head turned sideways so that the class could only see his profile. When he turned to face us, we saw that the left side of his face was missing. It had been blown away by a grenade in the trenches, he explained.

At night we covered up our windows so that the planes would not see the lights. There were air raids, with bombs exploding so close that I started to cry. My father always reassured me in a calm voice that all would be well.

In the summer, we were back on the farm. There was no telephone on the farm. News came from visitors or passersby. One afternoon some women who had been picking berries in the forest stopped by to see my grandmother. They sat in the courtyard and talked. This is the first time I heard about what later became known as the Holocaust. "They made them dig their own graves; they made them take off their clothes. Women held the hands of their children. They made them stand at the edge of the grave and shot them. Only one man fought back," one of the women told us.

Once, while on a visit to the farm, my father went for a walk and was stopped by a patrol. Later I overheard him tell my mother and grandmother that he had been questioned by the soldiers then told to turn around and keep walking. He had walked back expecting a bullet in the back of his head at any moment.

In addition to air combat, there were ground troops moving back and forth through our land, sometimes Russian, sometimes German. My brother and I would sit in deep grass, like rabbits, and watch the soldiers tramp through the farm. Mostly we saw their boots but once I caught the eye of a soldier and reaped a smile. At another time a group of German soldiers came through demanding "Speck, Butter, Eier" (bacon, butter, eggs). My brother decided to put a stop to this by raising the cow bar to block their passage through the courtyard. Immediately a soldier lowered a rifle at his chest.

My mother, who happened to be watching, started to scream, "Put it down, put it down!" After a tense moment, Neil disdainfully dropped the cow bar at their feet.

In the fall, my parents took my brother back to the city to attend school. My grandmother and I were left alone on the farm. One day I was playing on the sun porch when my grandmother rapidly entered the room, scooped up some pieces of the dried bread, and hurried out again. Shortly afterward she returned, her finger pressed against her lips, indicating silence, her other hand clutching a paring knife. She pressed her back against the wall next to the door, listening intently, the knife raised. We both held our breath, but there was only silence in the house.

A little later, she breathed a sigh of relief and said, chuckling, "I went out on the steps to throw out dishwater and tossed it on a soldier before I saw him. He stepped back in a hurry but got wet anyway, on the front. I gave him some bread. I wondered whether he might have followed me into the house."

The subject of fear was taboo with my mother and grandmother. They both had faced the greatest of fears, the annihilation of the self. However, as I encountered more horrid tales of mass murders, my sense of immortality began to slip away. I became the repository of secret, undefined fears.

One morning a strong wind was blowing from the west. After breakfast my grandmother urged me to go out and play. "Stay out of the wind. You'll get an earache. Play on the other side, where it is sunny," she admonished.

I took my dolls and set them up on the porch. Sometime later I glanced out to the field where the hay was stacked. One of the haystacks looked uneven. I saw what looked like some clothing. I quickly gathered up my dolls and went inside to the kitchen, where my grandmother was boiling jam in a large kettle and trying to stir down some pink foam. She ordered me back outside. I went to play on the windy side, where I was out of sight of the haystack. Immediately my grandmother came after me, scolding, "Didn't I tell you to stay out of the wind? Go back to the sunny side at once." Mute with fear, I went back to play on the porch. When I looked out at the haystack, I saw no one there.

At another time my grandmother said, "If someone comes and intends to harm you, just cover your face and turn away. Don't beg."

In the summer of 1944, as the Soviet army once again approached, there was talk in our family about leaving Latvia and heading for Sweden in a fishing boat, but there were reports of fishing boats being lost at sea. After a while my parents concluded that the risk to life was too great, and that project was scrapped.

On the morning of my ninth birthday, I woke up from a happy dream. I had dreamt about airmen coming down by parachutes and bringing me chocolate. The reality was quite different. My father came from the city and brought along a small can of pineapple rings. We ate this delicacy alone in the kitchen, like conspirators. I didn't know that we would soon be separated.

A few weeks later my parents arrived with a family my brother and I did not know. There were two children about the same age as my brother and myself, and we were eager for playmates. We took them on a walk along the borders of the property. When we returned to the farmhouse in the afternoon, my parents told us that my brother, mother, and I would be leaving on a boat for Germany the next day. From there we would proceed by train to Posen in Poland, where we would stay with Frau Weiss for a few months until the war was over.

While out walking with the newly arrived children I had gathered a bouquet of wildflowers, intending to give them to my father, whom I had not seen since my birthday. I was about to hand them to him when my grandmother reached for the bouquet, saying, "These are for grandmother." She was weeping. I didn't have the heart to tell her that the flowers were intended for my father. I gave the bouquet to my grandmother.

We stood in the kitchen saying good-bye. The new family was moving in with my grandmother so that she would not have to live alone. My grandmother was weeping. She kept repeating, "We'll never see each other again." My mother tried to pacify her by promising to return in three months, when the war was expected to be over. My grandmother was right. We never saw her again. The date was August 8, 1944. We left the farm in two horse-drawn carriages. My father and brother sat in the first one and my mother and I in the other.

That night in the city everything was packed away. I had to spend the night on the living-room couch without any sheets. I felt that it was an outrage to sleep without sheets and I threw a tantrum. I slept poorly. In the morning my father took us by horse cab to the harbor, where we said good-bye to him and to a cousin who had accompanied us. My father assured us that he would join us soon.

LEAVING LATVIA

The ship that would take us to Germany was too large to dock at the port of Riga. It waited for us out in the open sea. Passengers were brought to the waiting ship by a small boat that shuttled back and forth from the harbor in the city to the ship out at sea. The name of the ship was *Monte Rosa*, after the second-highest peak in the Alps.

My mother, brother, and I stood on the open deck of the small boat and watched the skyline of the city recede. A few minutes into the river journey my mother mentioned that we were now passing by Grandmother's farm, which was a few miles inland. For some unknown reason my brother and I started to weep. I wept from the depth of my heart with an overwhelming grief that I would experience only a few times in my life.

On the deck of the *Monte Rosa* we heard that the former president of Latvia, Kviesis, had died of a heart attack on board the ship. Since death had become a major preoccupation of mine, I wanted to see what a dead person would look like. I wandered through the many hallways of the ship and up and down the stairwells looking for the body. In the meantime, the body was transferred back to the small boat without my seeing it.

Anticipating danger had become a second nature to me, and I had braced myself for a *Titanic*-like disaster from air raids on our ship or from torpedoes fired from lurking submarines. However, nothing untoward happened, and after two days of calm seas we arrived in the German port of Gotenhafen.

That night, while we waited in the harbor for transportation to the train station, the harbor was bombed. I remember being carried by a panicked crowd into a truck, where we crammed ourselves in helter-skelter among pieces of luggage, grabbing at whatever was there to hold on to. Incandescent red target flares illuminated the night, and bombs exploded around us. The truck labored to its destination, much too slowly.

Then we were on a train and it was the middle of the night. I was angry about having to sleep sitting up all night in a crowded railroad car. My mother scolded me and told me to go sleep. I started to cry. At some point she became angry, yanked me to my feet, and dragged me to the other end of the car, where she admonished me for being a nuisance. I continued my protest. She spun me around and spanked my bottom while a carful of indifferent, sleep-starved refugees looked on. I howled even louder.

A young woman with medium-length hair who was seated by the window asked me to come and sit by her. She made space for me at the window and pointed to the night sky. The night was clear and there were stars everywhere. She pointed out some of the constellations, then asked, "How many stars do you think there are? Let's count them." That is the last thing I remember of the train ride. The unknown woman would eventually become the role model for my second career, clinical social work. Within our first month in Germany, I was to meet the role model for my first career.

We stayed with Frau Weiss in German-occupied Poland for two weeks. She lived alone in a modest apartment. Her daughter-in-law and her two grandchildren lived nearby. The grandchildren, two girls named Ingeborg and Assya, had been occasional playmates of ours in Latvia. I remember laughing myself to death in long tickling sessions with them.

I also remember Posen as the place where I told my first willful lie.

Frau Weiss had an heirloom sterling-silver hair-brush and ivory comb set. One day when everyone was gone, while I was home alone and bored, I examined the brush and comb. As I was running my fingers along the teeth of the comb, to my surprise, one of the teeth broke. I put the set back on the dresser. In the evening Frau Weiss and my mother asked me if I had broken the comb. Knowing that there were no witnesses and fearing severe punishment from Frau Weiss and my mother, I said what was in my best interests: "No." I absorbed some hard stares but didn't flinch. In telling this first conscious lie I felt a perverse sense of power.

The German government did not grant us permission to remain in occupied Poland. We had to move on to Germany. My mother, brother, and I went by train to Halle an der Saale, where we lived in a single room in an inexpensive hotel. The three of us slept in the same bed, with my mother in the middle. Using food coupons, we ate one meal daily, the noon meal, in a restaurant.

The cost of eating food in the restaurant was higher than cooking it at home, but we had no home. When we ran out of coupons, we ate kohlrabi soup at a food kitchen. My brother and I were as thin as scarecrows and we were beginning to outgrow our clothes. We must have looked pathetic. One day on the streets of Halle a German lady took notice of us. She invited my mother to cook at her home. Her name was Frau Engel.

My mother was not much of a cook, so Frau Engel did most of the cooking. I remember standing in the Engels' kitchen watching Frau Engel place a piece of coal in the oven. Her arm was covered with black coal dust up to her elbow. She was a serious young woman with light-brown hair. She did not use any makeup, not even lipstick.

The Engels had no children. Herr Engel was a scientist and teacher. In the evening, Herr Engel entertained my brother and me by doing magic tricks with coins. He also had a microscope at home and taught us how to use it. I remember looking at the root of my hair and being fascinated by the details. I wanted to be a scientist like Herr Engel when I grew up. I reached that goal when I graduated with a degree in chemistry from Brooklyn College a dozen years later.

My mother tried to persuade the Engel family to flee west, away from the advancing Russian army, but the Engels were convinced that Germany would win the war. Herr Engel talked about secret, powerful weapons being developed by the German military that would guarantee a German victory.

While in Halle we received a letter from my father. He wrote that he would leave Latvia at ten minutes to midnight. I got excited, expecting him to arrive in the next few days, and was disappointed when my mother explained that it was only a figure of speech.

My brother and I spent our time in Halle walking the streets. I remember seeing many brick-and-stone buildings and a sign that said, "Leipzig 30 km." One afternoon my brother and I were returning to the hotel by our usual route when suddenly, on the crowded street, we saw our father walking toward us. He was wearing his black winter coat. "Papa!" we shouted and rushed into his open arms.

CZECHOSLOVAKIA: WINTER AND SPRING OF 1944–45

I n October my father obtained permission for us to go to Prague, in Czechoslovakia. We were to spend the winter of 1944–45 in Czechoslovakia. We were settled into a stately private home in a small town outside Prague called Doschiechovitz. The owners of the large house, which was situated in a park-like setting, were Czech aristocrats by the name of Sudra. Now we were the intruders, refugees settled by the Germans in occupied Czech homes. The Sudras nonetheless treated us with courtesy.

The town was too small to have a school. That winter, my brother and I commuted by train to a school in another village. I remember running down the hill early in the morning to catch the train while it was still dark and seeing the train pull into the station, sparks flying high into the air from the coal-fueled engine. On several return trips the tracks ahead were bombed. The train would come to a halt, and an announcement was made in German: "Alle austeigen, zu Fuss weiter" (Everyone off, proceed on foot).

The house where we lived had a caretaker, an old woman named Vandzurova. Like my grandmother, Vandzurova wore a dark headscarf tied under her chin. One day, Vandzurova motioned for me to follow her into the basement, where she lived. The basement room was dark and drab. She motioned for me to sit down on a chair. I sat down. She cut a thick piece of dark bread, spread it generously with a liver pâté, and handed it to me. Then she sat down opposite me and smiled as she watched me eat.

Winter came early in Czechoslovakia that year. The first snow fell before the roses in the Sudra garden had finished blooming. My mother got so excited about seeing a rose in the snow that she wrote a poem about it. We had left Latvia in August without winter clothes. I was nine years old and growing.

Although I only had a light coat and no mittens, I spent hours playing in the snow. As a result, I got a painful frostbite on my fingers and caught a cold. As I lay sick in bed, Vandzurova fed me hot garlic broth, which was believed to cure fever and alleviate frostbite. I was sick a lot that winter. I lay on a cot in the corner of the room that had been allotted to us.

During that winter we made several cultural excursions. We went to Dresden because my parents wanted to see the art collection at the Zwinger. Dresden was believed to be safe from air raids. Most people in Germany believed that no one would dare to destroy the city's famous baroque architecture and art collections. I remember sitting on a streetcar in Dresden. I was sick and running a fever. A well-dressed German man asked me to get up and give my seat to his wife, who was not feeling well. I gave up my seat. Three months later the British leveled Dresden in a surprise air attack.

We visited the Goethe House in Weimar. It was a palatial home lacking in warmth. Goethe's death mask was displayed in the center of the lobby. I was cold and weak and lacked energy to continue with the tour. My parents knocked on the door of a nearby house and asked if I could wait inside. The lady did not appear enthused but let me sit on a chair in the dining room while my parents and brother continued to explore the Goethe House.

In the spring of 1945 we left Czechoslovakia and traveled west with a group of other Latvian refugees to get away the from approaching Soviet troops. At one point about a dozen of us, adults and children, were in an open truck near a train station. On either side of us were uniformed German troops retreating on foot and on bicycles. Two low-flying airplanes appeared in the sky, the sun behind them. There was no air-raid alarm or warning. Suddenly the planes took a dive and opened fire. I could see the airman with a machine gun aimed at the truck. The German soldiers along the side of the road dropped to the ground and blended in with the surrounding grass. Surprised, I marveled at the effectiveness of camouflage for a brief moment.

Panic ensued in the back of the truck. We pushed, shoved, jumped, and ran for the closest building. Our group crashed through a window and landed in someone's kitchen. A woman was inside, baking. A girl about my own age started to pray. I had never prayed out of fear and was embarrassed to admit that I was afraid, but I thought I had better join in or God would single me out for death. I started to say the Lord's Prayer. My father nudged me and took me over to the sink. There was a dirty cup with what appeared to be the remains of an egg yolk in it. My father took the cup, ran some water in it, and urged me to drink. I took a sip. I was in shock and don't remember what happened next.

My brother remembered the incident as follows: "As we entered the town of Asch, most of the traffic were German soldiers retreating toward the east. We saw a couple of airplanes preparing to dive and realized we better get off the truck and out of the way. We managed to get in a house through a basement window. I don't know if anyone was killed when the planes strafed the street."

We reached the town of Asch, a small German town on the Czech border, in April 1945. The Third Reich was in chaos. It was impossible to know to what military power we would be surrendering ourselves. Some said it would be the British, some thought we would meet up with the Americans, and others feared that the Russians had been gaining on us and would soon overrun us. In Asch we stayed indoors at a hotel listening for military action, but there was only silence. We stayed away from the windows for fear of being shot at.

Someone came running and reported having seen tanks in the street with stars on them. Panic spread through the hotel. Everyone thought the Russians had caught up with us. Then someone mentioned that the stars were white, not red. No one knew what country painted white stars on their military equipment. Someone said it was the Americans. Indeed, American troops had conquered Asch without a shot being fired. The city was occupied by the American troops on April 20, 1945. There was no resistance: the German army had melted away, and the only shots we saw fired involved the shooting out of a door lock in a house the American soldiers wanted to search.

We quickly found out that the Americans would soon be leaving, as the whole of Czechoslovakia was to be occupied by the Russians. Thus, we were soon on our way again.

I was getting in a truck to leave Asch when a black GI handed me a small, round, olive-colored tin can. The lid had been removed. Inside the can were chocolate and several clumps of what I now recognize as shredded wheat. I had never seen dry cereal before and was puzzled about what to do with it. I thanked him, and the truck took off.

The GI was one of many people during the war who offered me food. I was very thin and looked even skinnier wearing clothes that I had outgrown. When we started to live in displaced persons camps after the war, the physicians who evaluated the health of the children always prescribed me supplemental rations of chocolate.

"We arrived in Bayreuth in early May," my brother wrote. "We stayed on a farm south of the city. There were already some refugee families living there. I don't think we had to pay rent there[;] I think the authorities (whoever they were then) just put us up there. Mother, having grown up on a farm, helped with various chores, including milking the cows, and helping at the birth of a calf, so she was quite well liked by the owners."

My brother wrote about our mother's other talents: "My mother was a published author. To be specific, she was a poet and had three books of poetry published, two in Latvia and one in the [United States]. Her first volume of poetry came out in the late 1930s in independent Latvia, the second was published in 1942 while Latvia was under German occupation during World War II, and the last volume was published in 1961, in New York. Her poems were also published in various Latvian periodicals."

My brother continued in his memoir:

I think the awareness that my mother wrote poetry came sometime after I realized that she was a lawyer, although at that time I am not sure what a lawyer did. Poetry did not impress me[;] although I learned to read at an early age, it was prose that appealed to me—stories of danger and adventure. Poetry was stuff to be memorized and recited at school. I don't think I had appreciation for my mother's poems until my late teens. At one time my mother was working on a novel, which never came to be. The excerpts that I read were a lot more interesting than her verses. My first memories of my mother are of a stylish lady, who liked to sleep in late when possible. Later I also found out that she had other talents—she could milk cows and do various farm chores. All in all, she was a woman of multiple talents. She was also a rather impulsive person. She was married twice before she married my father when she was twenty-seven.

DISPLACED PERSONS CAMPS

The war ended in Europe on May 8, 1945. For six years after the war, we lived in various displaced persons (DP) camps in Germany. At first we lived in Wiesbaden in military barracks, then we were moved to Fulda and finally to Munich.

In Latvia, my brother and I had led isolated lives. Aside from the few contacts we made in school, there were no other playmates in our city house or on the farm. In the DP camps, for the first time in our lives we made friends with other children. I met my first girlfriend, Solveg, in Wiesbaden, in the girl scouts. She was a spunky girl, a year younger than me, with dark hair that she wore in braids. Once when other girls ganged up on me and were harassing me for wearing dirty clothes, Solveg joined them. Hurt, I ran home. Sometime later Solveg came to me and apologized for turning on me. I was flabbergasted. No one ever had apologized to me before.

After about a year and a half, the camp in Wiesbaden was liquidated. Solveg and her family went to Belgium, where her father had been offered a job as a coal miner. I found this out much later, after our family had moved to the United States and Solveg's family had left Belgium for Canada. The next time I saw her was in Toronto at a Latvian folk festival when I lived in New York. Some Latvian girl-friends and I had decided to attend the festival in Toronto and had gone there on a Greyhound bus. Our family, meanwhile, was moved to Fulda, where we spent two years. In Fulda I experienced the first big crush of my life. I was twelve years old.

The object of my affection was a boy I saw in the window on my way home from school. He was leaning on his elbows and called my name as I passed by. Every time I walked home he was there, calling my name. I would stop, stick out my tongue at him, and continue on my way. I learned from friends that his name was Antons Skapars.

Antons had dark hair and brown eyes and was eighteen years old. I would frequently see him out playing volleyball with older girls and boys. However, when he saw me he would call me over and show me how to hit a serve. He told my friends that I had beautiful eyes and that he wished that I were sixteen. I started to daydream about Antons. I drew interlinking hearts on the covers of my schoolbooks, with arrows piercing the hearts. Once, in a dark washroom of the barracks, he tried to kiss me, but my mother materialized out of nowhere and yanked me away.

When the Fulda camp was downsized a few years later and our family was assigned to a camp in Munich, Antons came to the train station to see me off. As the train pulled out of the station, I started to weep. Again, the tears came from a place deep within me. I wept uncontrollably, like I had wept on the boat when we left Latvia.

At the DP camp in Munich, we were again housed in military barracks on the outskirts of the town. In Munich I met Laila, who became my closest friend. Her parents had known my parents in Latvia. When we arrived in Munich, my parents went to visit Laila's parents, who already lived in the camp. Laila's parents sent her downstairs to the courtyard, where I was by myself. She was twelve at the time and I was thirteen. The first time I saw her, she wore her light-brown hair in two long braids tied with white ribbons. She was very poised as she introduced herself. We started talking. In a short period of time we became the best of friends.

HOPELESS AND HELPLESS

Thanks to my mother's restless, searching nature, we were able to come to the United States. Due to my father's advanced age (he was seventeen years older than my mother) and to the fact that my brother and I were still too young to be considered employable, no country that was taking in refugees was willing to accept our family, and so our family lingered for six years in DP camps in postwar Germany . We applied to go to Canada, and after we were rejected by Canada, we applied to go to Australia. I still remember the interview at the Australian consulate. We had to travel from Munich to Frankfurt by train for the appointment.

The Australian deputy consul was a young red-haired man in his early thirties who sat behind a desk with his feet up in a narrow room. He did not get up to greet us or to shake our hands. He looked over our family and, without asking a single question, dismissed us with the shake of his head. We returned to the Munich DP camp hopeless and helpless.

The only country we had not yet applied to was the United States. We did not believe we stood a chance of being accepted there. We had no job skills to offer. We knew that the United States accepted only young people or people with technical skills, such as engineers, dentists, and doctors. People with legal skills like my parents were of no interest to the United States.

My mother refused to give up and steered our family in the right direction. She started to take English lessons at the Quaker library located in the Munich DP camp where we resided. She even brought home a book in English for me to read, *The Lost Horizon* by James Hilton. It described a mythical place in the mountains of Asia where people do not grow old. It was the first book I read in English, and it left a deep impression on me. I had to struggle through it with a limited English vocabulary. What kept me going were the story line and its magical setting. I was fourteen years old when I read it, on my camp cot, leaning on my elbow. My brother read several books, but he remembered only one. He wrote, "I only remember one book from that time. It was *Uncle Tom's Cabin*. That was a gripping story, the first book that grabbed me emotionally."

During the years in Germany, my parents worked in various capacities at the DP camps. My mother taught Latvian at the DP camp high school. My father served on various committees. Once I heard my father tell my mother that he got only one vote on a committee.

"Someone must have voted for you," my mother said. My father explained that he had cast the vote for himself. My heart ached.

The summers were the best parts of my time in Germany. For the refugee children the YMCA organized summer camps by scenic lakes, places in Germany that my family could never have afforded to visit. These camps were multinational and included children refugees from all Eastern European countries. At campfires in the evenings, each nationality put on performances of songs and dance. I was most impressed with the Hungarian and Ukrainian dancers.

Many families from the DP camps were emigrating to Great Britain, Canada, the United States, and Australia. The Latvian population in the Munich DP camp dwindled, and the Latvian school was closed.

Laila and I started to attend a German high school in Munich. It was a major adjustment because up until now our schooling had been in Latvian. I studied English, French, and German at the high school, while I continued to speak Latvian at home. Food and money were in short supply. My parents had no paying jobs. I was always hungry. In Munich, my school lunches consisted of one plain roll of white bread with nothing on it.

Food was always on my mind. I remember a time when I went with some friends to a swimming pool a few miles from the refugee camp. I became so hungry that I decided to leave early because I could not stop thinking of the little piece of cheese wrapped in tin foil that I knew was in the cupboard. We had no refrigerators. All the way home I thought of the cheese. When I got home, it was still there. I took off the foil and broke it open. It was full of maggots.

We applied to go to Canada and Australia but these countries would not accept a family with children who could not yet work and parents who had no technical skills. My father was already past sixty.

My mother wrote for help to friends who had emigrated to the United States. In the late 1940s and early 1950s, the United States required a $1,000 guarantee from a US sponsor for a refugee family to enter the country. Our friends, who had recently emigrated, did not have the spare money to help us. However, my mother struck up a friendship with an American Quaker woman who worked at the DP camp library and taught English there. This lady found a Quaker community in the United States who were willing to post the $1,000 for our family. This made us eligible to apply to come to the United States. The Quaker community of the Philadelphia suburb of Abington became our sponsors and enabled our family to finally leave the war behind.

AMERICA

On April 23, 1951, we boarded the American military transport ship *General SS Stewart* in Bremerhaven, Germany, for the trip to the United States. There were several hundred refugees of different nationalities on board, all heading for the same destination, New York City. I was fifteen years old.

On the ship we slept in bunk beds in the galley. I could hear people moan from seasickness. I was determined not to get seasick. To keep myself occupied, I volunteered in the cafeteria to help mothers with small children carry their trays. I did not get seasick, but quite a few others did. On the morning of our arrival in the United States, we stood at the railing looking at New York City and the Statue of Liberty. I was mesmerized by the many cars moving on the shore and inadvertently put my gloved hand in someone's vomit. I pulled off my gloves and tossed them overboard. It was May 2, 1951.

No one met us in New York upon our arrival. We were directed to a waiting lounge by immigration authorities to wait for our name to be called. After we were cleared for entry, we waited again for our name to be called for further instructions. Eventually we were transferred to the 34th Street Station, where we waited again for a train, this one to Trenton, New Jersey.

It was dark by the time we got off the train in Trenton. A Quaker lady named Mrs. Chase met us at the station and drove us to her home in Bryn Gweled, Pennsylvania, for supper. I remember a large bowl of potato chips on the table. I thought they were fried potatoes that had grown cold while waiting for our arrival.

After supper my parents were invited to go next door to meet Mr. and Mrs. Romberg, who were our sponsors. My brother and I stayed at the Chase home by ourselves. The phone rang. I hesitated, then picked it up, butterflies in my stomach. It was for us. One of the Romberg children was calling to invite my brother and me to come over to play ball. After

I hung up I could hardly believe that I had handled a phone call successfully, in English, on my first day in America.

The following day we went with our sponsors to Philadelphia. Mrs. Romberg dropped me and my brother off at Wanamaker's department store while the adults went to attend to some kind of business. The place was like a museum to me. It was full of beautiful things, but nothing was available because I had no money. Later that day, my brother and I took the subway on our own. We went to look up some of my brother's friends, who had immigrated before us and lived in Philadelphia. We got off the subway and were walking on the street looking for the address when we saw my brother's friend, Gene, walking toward us. It was a happy reunion. Again, I was amazed by our ability to find our way around Philadelphia all on our own and accomplish what we had set out to do on our second day in America.

On Sunday we went with our sponsors to a Quaker meeting. There was no altar nor minister nor priest. People sat in stern silence. After a period of contemplation, someone got up and talked, and then someone else did the same thing. On Monday I was sent to live with a Quaker family, the Newtons. The Newtons had a girl a few years younger than me, named Jessica. I was to attend a private Quaker girls school, the Abington Friends School, with Jessica for the remainder of the school year. In school I felt lost. I thought I would just coast for the last few weeks of the term. When I made no effort, I was assigned a tutor, who actually sat with me in the library and expected me to do some work.

At the Newtons' home, I ate rich American food, food that I had never tasted in my life. My stomach protested. I threw up. My nose also got all stuffy—it was probably the pollen, but I had never heard of allergies and I thought I had a cold. I went to bed and stayed there. After a few days, Mrs. Newton came to me and suggested that I might want to get up and take a bath. I was horrified. In Europe we took baths once a week, and never when we had colds. I declined her offer.

By early summer we all had jobs, which our sponsors had found for us. My father worked in the greenhouse of the Tinari African violet farm, where he propagated and took care of the new plants. He earned sixty-five cents per hour. My mother was cleaning houses in Bryn Athyn. My brother was employed as a gas station attendant in Huntington Valley, Pennsylvania, and I was sent off to Gettysburg to work in the kitchen and wait on tables at a Lutheran church's summer camp. I received fifteen dollars per week. Our sponsors kept my money in trust. I was given two dollars per week for personal use. I turned sixteen while waiting on tables at the camp.

Almost from the day I arrived in America I was separated from my family. All my communication from then on was in English. By the end of the summer I was fluent in English.

In September I enrolled in the eleventh grade at Lower Moreland High School in Huntington Valley. I excelled in math and French but flunked physics during my first semester. I repeated the course and got an A in the spring. In school I made my first American friend. Her name was Evelyn. We took long walks together on the railroad tracks that went through the town. I think that if we had stayed in Pennsylvania and I had continued school there I would have made a relatively easy adjustment to life in America. But it was not to be.

In the fall of 1952 my parents decided to move to New York City. In Pennsylvania they felt socially isolated. New York was teeming with Latvian immigrants. There was a Latvian network that helped other Latvians to find jobs. The Latvians had figured out a system that was workable and brought in enough income to survive. Most men without language skills took jobs as building superintendents in Brooklyn. They became known as "supers." In exchange they got a free apartment and a small salary. Women went to work outside the home.

The Latvian network found a job for my father as a super on 53rd Street in Brooklyn. However, he was still bound by a contract at the Tinari African violet farm. My parents decided that I had to go to New York and take the apartment and the job on the behalf of my father and hold it for him until he was able to relocate.

I arrived in New York City by bus in September 1952. From the bus station, I took a subway to the designated station in Brooklyn. I carried my belongings with me in a bundle. I went to pick up the key from a Latvian super, then went to the designated address on 53rd Street. It was a six-story apartment building in a lower-middle-class neighborhood of Brooklyn, not far from Coney Island. The super's apartment, the only apartment in the basement, was behind the boiler. The basement smelled of cat urine. The apartment had no furniture and no drapes. There was a mattress on the floor of the bedroom. I put my bundle on the mattress and sat down. When night came I turned on the solitary light bulb that hung from the ceiling. I could see the feet of the passers-by in the street. Then it occurred to me that people could look in and see me alone in the basement apartment. I turned off the light and sat on the mattress in the dark. I spent about two weeks living alone there. During the day I placed garbage cans on the curb, swept the sidewalk, and collected rent. It was one of the loneliest and scariest times of my life.

One day, when I was dragging garbage cans back from the curb, a middle-aged woman who lived in the apartment building asked me, "Why aren't you in school?" I had focused so hard on my safety and survival in the city that I had forgotten all about school. I had no idea where I should go to school. I asked her to tell me where the school was located. She directed me to the New Utrecht High School in Brooklyn. The school year had already started. I went to see the principal but I had no school records with me. It was a question of what grade I should attend. By then I had already attended twelve different schools in ten years in three different languages. I told the principal that I wanted to stay with my age group and graduate the following spring. He agreed to let me stay with my age group. I was seventeen years old. New Utrecht was a large, impersonal school with ten thousand students.

At the end of the first semester, the homeroom teacher announced the students who had the highest grade-point average. I was surprised when I heard that another student and I shared the top spot. I graduated from New Utrecht High in June 1953 in the upper 10 percent of the class. My German teacher, Rebecca Bridge, had taken a special interest in me. When I graduated, she gave me a copy

of the poems of Heinrich Heine in English transla-
tion. Following graduation from New Utrecht High
School, I was accepted at Brooklyn College.

COLLEGE YEARS

Not knowing what I wanted to major in, I signed up for the experimental curriculum at Brooklyn College. This curriculum offered concentrated courses in all areas of college study during the first two years. I was frightened of science because of my early failure in physics, but I gained some confidence when I got an A in a biology class.

I agonized about my major over solitary lunches in a small garden on the campus, where I had a squirrel for company. I had many interests but no compelling passions. Knowing what to major in required some self-knowledge and self-confidence, and I felt I lacked in both. I felt drawn to psychology in the hope that it would help me understand myself better, but part of me was afraid of what I might find out. I didn't know how to type, and the prospect of writing long term papers in English overwhelmed me. Technical skills were in demand, however, and were transferable from one society to another. At the end of my sophomore year I decided to major in chemistry. It would give me a technical skill while keeping a door open for a future in medicine.

During summers I worked as a waitress with my friend Zinta at various resorts in New York state. We picked lovely locations where it was cool and green to work. One summer we worked at a resort in upstate New York on Schroon Lake. I remember this summer most for my intense romance with a boy named Donny. Donny worked as camp counselor at a boys camp across the lake. Every night he came across the lake in his motor boat to see me. We spent the nights necking on the beach. We must have necked right through the Perseid meteorite shower for I had never before seen so many shooting stars. Another summer we worked at the Lake Mohonk Mountain House resort in New Paltz, New York. This famous resort is described by Gail Goodwin in her novel *The Finishing School.*

My brother had dropped out of college in Ohio and had come to join us in New York. For a while the four of us lived in a one-bedroom apartment in Brooklyn. My father and brother slept in the living room while my mother and I shared the bedroom. My parents were heavy smokers and our little Brooklyn apartment was always filled with smoke.

By my junior year in college my mother had obtained a job in the Columbia University library in order to get free tuition to study at Columbia for a master's degree in library science. She was also going through menopause.

During my junior year in college my mother started to complain about not being able to sleep. She would put the light on at odd hours of the night, light a cigarette, and repeat over and over, "I can't sleep." Once, when she was out of cigarettes, she got up at 3:00 a.m. and walked to the nearest subway station, where there was an all-night newspaper stand, to buy cigarettes.

My mother continued to go to work despite not being able to sleep. Soon she stopped bathing and changing her clothes. Each morning she left the house wearing the same clothes she had worn all week, her hair unwashed and with runs in her stockings. A Latvian doctor prescribed her the sleeping pill Doriden, which is no longer on the market.

One day, in the women's restroom at Brooklyn College a girl I did not know said to me, "You look as tired as I feel." I looked in the mirror, and indeed my face looked haggard and drawn, but not feeling rested felt normal to me. In retrospect I realize that I had not experienced a sense of well-being for so long that I had forgotten what a normal mood felt like.

That summer I was waiting tables at a resort located on Schroon Lake in upstate New York. One day I received a phone call from Columbia University informing me that they had to let my mother go. The lady who called me seemed quite concerned about my mother and suggested that I return to the city to care for her. My brother was in the military in Maryland, and with my mother unemployed I was the only person in the family with a job. This was long before "depression" had become a household word, long before the days of Prozac. I was frightened by my mother's mental decline but didn't know what to do about it. My father was at home and her close male friend Otto was nearby. I thanked her for the information and hung up. I remained upstate and worked through the summer. I felt cowardly but an instinct of self-preservation told me to stay where I was. I had taken my mother's hand as a small child when she had lamented that no one wanted to hold her hand when crossing a street on a Sunday outing together with my father and brother. At age twenty, as an adult woman, I lacked the capacity to do so.

In the fall my mother wasn't any better. The doctor recommended electroshock therapy. We didn't know anything about it. We had no health insurance. One of the Latvian women we knew worked for a psychiatrist who administered electroshock therapy in his office for twenty-five dollars. My mother went to see him. After he administered the shock, she took the subway home. She got lost. Eventually she made her way home. From then on, my father accompanied her on her visits.

Slowly, my mother emerged from her depression. She gave up the idea of graduate school and took a clerical job with a French perfume company by the name of Houbigant, the makers of Chantilly perfume. She worked for the company till the day she died.

I began to have sleep problems myself. I slept only about three or four hours a night. I felt surrounded by dread. My strong mother had fallen apart. Keeping physically active by waitressing in a fresh-air resort during the summer with a school friend for company, I knew that I could keep going, but if I returned to New York I would fall apart along with my mother.

In the fall, when I returned to the city to complete my last year of studies as a chemistry major at Brooklyn College, the word had gotten around the Latvian refugee subculture in New York that my mother was unable to work. My mother's friends stepped in with help and advice. We had no knowledge of psychiatric illnesses or the doctors who treated them. I was in my senior year at Brooklyn College. Brooklyn College was a commuter school. I spent my days at the college or at the Brooklyn public library where I did most of my studying. My brother partially supported the family with a job in the construction industry on Long Island. At that time there was a construction boom on Long Island. A Latvian entrepreneur was building houses and hired young Latvian men to work for his building projects. It was the Latvian immigrant network that helped us survive the early years in the United States.

ROCKEFELLER INSTITUTE

In the meantime, I graduated from Brooklyn College with a BS in chemistry and went job hunting in my field. My first choices were the drug companies, which paid high salaries. However, when I did not get a callback after an interview at Pfizer, I started to check out the better-known hospital labs. In those days a job hunter walked into the personnel office and made inquiries. There were several major hospitals on the Upper East Side of New York, near the East River, and that is where I went looking.

On a sunny day in October 1957, I walked into the personnel office of the Memorial Sloan Kettering Cancer Institute, located on East 60th Street in

Manhattan, and was sent up to a lab for an interview. I was offered a job there but did not like the idea that I would have to work every other Saturday. Down the street, between York Avenue and the East River, was the giant New York Hospital–Cornell Medical Center complex, and next to it was another potential employer, the Rockefeller Institute for Medical Research, currently known as Rockefeller University. The Rockefeller Institute had not been on my list, but then I remembered that an Estonian girl named Inge whom I knew from Brooklyn College had found a job in a research lab there. On an impulse, I decided to drop in the personnel office at Rockefeller. It was a fateful decision. After a brief interview at the personnel office I was sent to the lab of Dr. Bruce Merrifield, who had the open position. Dr. Merrifield worked on peptide synthesis. At the time of my interview I had no idea of his research interests. At one point during the interview he asked me what area of chemistry I was most interested in.

"Synthesis," I replied promptly.

I think I was offered a job there because I knew what I was interested in and our interests overlapped. The two of us worked side-by-side at the lab bench. Bruce Merrifield would go on to win the 1984 Nobel Prize in Chemistry for the development of a new method of protein synthesis. I worked with him on the very beginning stages of this project.

Once I started working at Rockefeller, our situation at home improved. I contributed to rent and household expenses, and my father was able to retire. We moved from the dark, ground floor, one-bedroom apartment to an apartment on the fourth floor with lots of light and a room for each of us. By then my brother had gotten married and moved out.

At a Christmas party at Rockefeller I met my future husband, John Hershey. I had not wanted to go to the party, but my Estonian friend Inge persuaded me to attend it with her. "Just for a little while," she insisted. On some level the "little while" became a lifetime.

The party room, with a richly decorated Christmas tree, overlooked the East River. It was cocktail hour. Small boats and barges with lights were passing below. Waiters walked among the guests with trays loaded with appetizers and drinks. Two young men made their way through the crowd toward Inge and me. I had met one of them, John Hershey, earlier in the day when he had stopped by the lab where I worked with Dr. Merrifield to talk about the project we were working on. He was a graduate student looking for a thesis-project sponsor. The other man was Robert Traut, also a graduate student, who was already working on his thesis under the Nobel Prize winner Fritz Lipmann. In seven years I had come from deprived living conditions in DP camps to a haven of wealth and fame.

In January, John joined the lab where Inge and I worked. From time to time, he would stop at my lab bench to chat. He had spent two years in Austria in alternative service as a conscious objector, where he had also learned how to ski. He had also visited Russia. We had much to talk about.

In February of 1959, I started to date John Hershey. At Christmas of that year, we got engaged at his parents' home in Lititz, Pennsylvania. It was a season of lights, social events, and candlelight church services. I had a sparkling diamond on my finger, but inside I felt jittery and uneasy. This psychological discomfort grew. I mentioned it to John.

"Maybe we can help each other," he said. I felt understood and comforted.

Accepting the position at the Rockefeller Institute was for me a life-changing decision. It opened a door to a world I had never expected to be part of. At Rockefeller I met the world's top scientists. And I met my future husband.

Bruce Merrifield would succeed in solid-phase protein synthesis. By 1963 he had automated the process. In 1984 he would be awarded the Nobel Prize in Chemistry for this achievement. It was a project that I had worked on in its very early stages. Following Merrifield's protocols I would synthesize small peptides that we hoped would act as enzymes. In his autobiography, *Life during a Golden Age of Peptide Chemistry*, published by the American Chemical Society in 1993, he gave credit to his technical staff, including me, for assistance with the project.

However, entering a rarified world peopled by top-notch intellectuals had its downside. Suddenly I was caught up in a lifestyle that I had not experienced since becoming an adult. I had grown up in deprivation in DP camps, lived in basement apartments in Brooklyn, had been reprimanded by a Chinese laundry worker for bringing in sheets in that were too dirty by his standards because our family could not afford laundry services very often. My early years of growing up in a privileged and socially prominent family in Latvia gave me some confidence, but there were times when I felt out of place.

I felt nervous about the upcoming marriage to a man from the American middle class, a very intelligent man on a full graduate scholarship at Rockefeller. I had met his parents, who belonged to a fundamentalist church, the Church of Brethren, in small-town Pennsylvania, which was so very different from my worldly European family, who now struggled to make ends meet in America with menial jobs.

John wanted a big wedding because both his sister and brother had had shotgun weddings. John, the good child, wanted to deliver the dreams of a white wedding to his parents, after his siblings had failed. John wanted a Trinidadian steel band at the wedding. We had been going to Smalls Paradise in Harlem to dance on some of our date nights, and John wanted to import this cool scene to his fellow students and co-workers at Rockefeller. I wanted a very small and private wedding. That was all I felt I could handle.

Three months before our scheduled wedding, my father died suddenly one night from a heart attack. I found him early one morning sitting on his bed, still fully dressed, his head leaning against the wall. I noticed a small grease spot on the wall where his head rested. An emotion that resembled both dread and excitement gripped me. It was the end of a world, his world. I knew he was dead even before I checked his pulse. I once had read about a minister who worked in an airport. He had no congregation or church. He said he ministered through his presence. Father had held the family together through his presence.

He was the first member of my immediate family to die. I was invaded by a sense of the insignificance of an individual's life in the larger context of this world. The suddenness of his end was a shock. I started to develop the same symptoms that my mother had displayed a few years ago, notably insomnia, agitation, and a preoccupation with the meaning of life.

The night after my father died I asked my mother if I could sleep with her. I needed to be next to her warm body. She let me sleep with her and shared her sleeping pills with me. Doriden worked for a few weeks, then it stopped working. I tried to add alcohol to the drug and that worked for a few nights. Then, in addition to insomnia and nihilistic thoughts, I started to have difficulty concentrating. I went to see my mother's doctor. He told me I was supposed to be happy. I was getting married. I should go to a good movie with my fiancé. We saw a movie entitled *I'm All Right, Jack*, but it did not improve my mood.

It was springtime in New York City. I noticed trees with pink blossoms on the Rockefeller grounds and wondered why I felt no pleasure in seeing them. I felt no pleasure at all. In fact, life to me felt totally drained of any hope, pleasure, or energy. I had not heard of depression and did not know what it was. All I was aware of was that something terrible was happening to me and I was helpless in the face of it.

Underlying the depression was agitation. I felt compelled to move. I would move from my mother's house to my brother's place and a few days later to John's apartment. John was rooming with Robert in an apartment on the west side of Central Park. Robert too was a graduate student at Rockefeller.

Robert noticed the changes in me and contacted another graduate student, a medical doctor who was working on his PhD. This student doctor recommended a psychiatrist for me. Later Robert told me that his father had crashed for a period of time in the middle of his adult life. Robert had recognized the symptoms of a severe depression.

As recommended, I went to see Dr. Anderson, a psychiatrist whose office was near Rockefeller. Dr. Anderson asked me questions such as how old was I, and whether I was taking any medications. I told him about Doriden. He said he could not evaluate me while I was on medication. He told me to stop taking it and come back in a few days for another evaluation.

The Doriden had suppressed my fear, and when I went off it cold turkey I experienced a terrific rebound characterized by extreme panic. Dr. Anderson hospitalized me briefly and put me on the antianxiety drug Librium. A severely depressed state that resembled mine was later described by William Styron in *Darkness Visible*, a wonderful book that had yet to be written. My depression was preceded by disturbed sleep. My recovery also arrived in sleep, at night, and was preceded by my first coherent dream in several months. In my dream I was sitting in a hay wagon that was being pulled by a horse. Dr. Anderson was sitting in the driver's seat, holding the reins.

Gradually, my sleep pattern improved. Over several weeks I returned to my normal self. Now I had to face the world. If I had not received prompt medical intervention as a result of working in an enlightened workplace, I might have ended up like my mother did by being fired and taking months to recover.

Having experienced a psychological crisis was frightening and stigmatizing. I did not know if my relationship to John could survive such an episode. I myself was not certain of the next step in my life. One day, during the lunch hour, I walked into a small neighborhood church. I just sat there until I felt a measure of peace. I surrendered myself to fate.

At about this point, Bruce Merrifield approached John and volunteered that a person in his immediate family had experienced a very similar episode in response to a stressful life event and recovered completely to lead a normal and productive life. This knowledge gave me hope. I felt accepted as a normal person by the Merrifield family.

Initially John and I had planned to marry on May 14. Instead we married a month later, on June 17, 1960. Only my mother, my brother, and my brother's wife, Ingeborg, were present at the small wedding performed in my mother's apartment by the Lutheran minister of the Latvian church. Instead of taking a western trip, we took a weekend honeymoon at a motel in nearby Connecticut.

John was born in Lancaster, Pennsylvania, on January 27, 1934. The family lived in Lititz, about ten miles from Lancaster in Pennsylvania Dutch country. His parents were middle class and belonged to the Church of Brethren. The family lived in a green two-story wood-frame house on a corner lot in a quiet residential neighborhood. Behind the house were cornfields.

John was the middle of three children. He had an older sister, Mary Lou, and a younger brother, Robert. In looks all three children resembled their mother, who was dark haired and had brown eyes. John's father was fair haired and had blue eyes. When John was seven years old his appendix ruptured. He was saved by his sister, who promptly notified John's mother. "Buddy is all doubled over from pain," she said. Buddy was John's nickname as a child. In the hospital John was saved by the surgeon and sulfa drugs.

John's father was a partner in an insurance company called Hershey and Gibbel. The two-story stone office building was the most imposing structure in downtown Lititz. On the outskirts of the town a subsidiary of the Nestle Company, named Wilbur, made chocolate. When I started to visit Lititz, the town frequently smelled of chocolate.

Church played a large role in the lives in John's family. The Brethren were Anabaptists who did not christen their children in infancy. Rather, at age twelve, a child could choose to be baptized or not. John later told me that there was great pressure to choose baptism. The Brethren followed biblical instructions for baptism: "He rose forthwith out of the water." This was interpreted as a need for total submersion and coming up face first. John participated in church activities until he went away to college at Haverford, Pennsylvania, where he met Robert.

In college John majored in chemistry, like Robert. During the first year, John roomed with a college-designated room-mate, who happened to be one of the princes of Thailand. During his second year he roomed with Rob. At the end of his second year of college, John became a conscientious objector and took a two-year leave of absence. He served his two years of alternative service in Linz, Austria, where he learned to ski and became friends with an Austrian family named Boehme. Mrs. Boehme worked as a secretary for the organization that John worked for. At the end of his stay in Austria John traveled through Greece and Egypt and then on to Palestine and Lebanon, where his aunt and uncle were living. There, he was met by their sons, James and Peter, and traveled together with them back to Austria. Somewhere along the way on this trip, John contracted hepatitis. By the time he returned to Austria, he was exhausted, his skin and eyes were yellow, and he was passing dark urine. Frau Bohme took charge and promptly hospitalized him. He spent several weeks in the hospital but eventually recovered. When he returned to college in the fall, he was still feeling the aftereffects of the illness. In his first two years in college he was a cross-country runner. When he tried to return to the sport, he found it difficult to run any distance at all.

After graduating with honors from Haverford College, John applied to graduate school at Rockefeller University in New York. At that time it was known as the Rockefeller Institute for Medical Research. It had no undergraduate program and only accepted graduate students. All students were on full Rockefeller scholarships. Robert, who had graduated from Haverford two years before John, was already a graduate student at Rockefeller. When I met John and Rob, they were room-mates in an off-campus apartment on the west side of Central Park. To get to work they had to walk through Central Park to the East River, where Rockefeller University was located.

WESTERN TRIP

In 1961 John and I took a six-week western trip. Our aim was to go all the way across the country to the Pacific Ocean and see the National Parks on the way. We traveled in John's old Chevrolet, which required more oil than gas. We camped most nights. Our first big attraction was Cape Hatteras, where we camped on the beach. I remember cooking lamb chops on the camp stove and then dropping them inadvertently in the sand. From there we drove west through North Carolina. I had seen slums in New York City but never such poverty in a rural area. We passed shack after shack inhabited by black people. We continued through the southern states first because it was early June. In the north we could encounter snow.

Eventually we came to the Grand Canyon, where we camped on the South Rim. We had a fight there. In anger, I started down the Bright Angel Trail. John came after me. Down and down we went with only one canteen of water between us. We came to Indian Springs, a green oasis among the red rocks. There was drinking water available. We filled up the canteen. At that point any sane person would have started back up, but we continued down, down, down until we reached the Colorado River at the bottom of the canyon. We were eight miles and seven thousand feet away from where we had started, and it was already afternoon. There were no other people around. We had only a brief moment to put our aching feet in the cold river before starting up. It was the hardest climb of my life. We zigzagged up and up on the dusty red trail, stopping now and then to catch our breath. By the time we reached the top, it was cold and dark. My whole body was trembling.

That night we ate at the restaurant in the lodge on the rim. We slept in our tent, but our bodies ached too much to get decent sleep. I did not know yet that I was already two months pregnant.

From the Grand Canyon we continued on to Yosemite. Bruce Merrifield had told us that we should see the Tuolumne Meadows. We decided to backpack in and camp by a lake in the meadows and then climb some peaks the next day. It was still June and there was snow in the meadows. I was not aware of the altitude of the meadows. All I knew was that I felt totally bushed. The next day I did not complete the climb of the peak. I turned back to our camp.

I had been to San Francisco before with my first boyfriend, Ed, and had told John what a wonderful city it was. Unfortunately, when we got there, the city was experiencing a heat wave. Most places in San Francisco did not have air conditioning. John was unhappy with the city. I did, however, take time out to get my hair done. Then we pushed north toward Oregon and Crater Lake. The heat spell continued through our trip north. Then we started to climb up toward the lake. Up and up we went. With each turn in the road the temperature dropped. We put on more clothes and then more clothes. By the time we reached the lake, we had to camp in snow again.

On the way home we visited Glacier National Park. We camped in the designated campground. When I got up to go to the bathroom during the night, I almost bumped into a bear as it was passing the tent. This did not stop us from backpacking in seven miles to Lake Solitude the next day. We went through Yellowstone National Park, camped in the Tetons by Jenny Lake, and took a mountain-climbing class.

My son John was born at the New York Hospital–Cornell Medical Center. My mother-in-law Mayno Hershey came to care for him and me for about a week after I came home from the hospital. By that time we had moved into a cockroach-infested apartment on East 83rd Street, just off York Avenue, near the Gracie Mansion. While I was at the hospital, my husband repainted the ugly pink-and-green apartment to a pleasing cream color. He had gotten rid of most of the cockroaches.

John received his PhD in biochemistry from the Rockefeller Institute in June 1963. By then I was already pregnant with our second child, Peter, who would be born in Cambridge, England. John applied for and received a Jane Coffin Child Fellowship to do postdoctoral studies at Cambridge University in England.

We left for England on July 2, 1963, on a Holland America Line ship named *New Amsterdam*. During the passage we placed Johnny in the ship's day-care center for part of the day while I read a biography about Tolstoy's wife, Sophia. We disembarked in Southampton, England, where a brand-new baby blue Hillman Minx was waiting for us. John drove us to Cambridge, where we temporarily stayed with Robert and his wife, Sheila, at a house on Barton Road while we looked for a house to rent. We found a lovely old house with a fireplace, a baby grand piano, and stained-glass windows in the hallway. However, the house would not become available until the fall. We would be able to move in in early September.

We could not stay with the Rob and Sheila for the balance of the summer, so we bought a portable crib for Johnny that could fit in the back seat of the Hillman and took off for the Continent. It was a rainy summer in Europe. We frequently camped out of necessity. John and I slept in a small pup tent, while Johnny slept in the car next to our tent. It was a challenge changing diapers while traveling, camping out, and being pregnant. In Bavaria, in southern Germany, we camped next to a gasthaus; men came out to pee near our tent after drinking their beer at the bar. In Switzerland we missed seeing the Alps due to constant rain. The weather improved somewhat in Austria, where John had friends that he had made while he did alternative service as a conscientious objector for two years before he came to do graduate work at Rockefeller. There we camped on the patio of John's friends, the Boehmes, while Johnny continued to sleep in the crib set up in the car in their driveway.

From Austria we went to Italy to attend the wedding of the son of John's parents' friends the Minichs. Paul Minich was marrying the daughter of the British consul. The reception was held at one of Peggy Guggenheim's homes, which was situated on a canal. We had to park our car outside the city. The car park was jammed. When we returned to it a few days later, it was the only car in the giant lot. We never found out where everyone had gone.

CAMBRIDGE, ENGLAND

During the first week in September we moved into our rented house on Cavendish Avenue. It was a furnished two-story brick duplex. It was not centrally heated. In the back there was a garden with pear trees. It was just a block off Hills Road, a major artery into downtown Cambridge.

We hired an au pair girl Denmark, Merete, to help with the children. In early November I was to give birth to our second child. Merete was a personable eighteen year old. Part of the day she attended English language classes downtown. She became a good mother substitute for Johnny.

In October, Sheila and Rob gave a party where we met new friends. Later in October my membranes broke, but labor did not start. I was hospitalized for about two weeks and given pitocin to induce labor, but still it did not start. The attending physician scheduled a Cesarean for November 10 to teach medical students the procedure. This scared me, and I went spontaneously into labor. On November 9, our second son, Peter, was born. It was a long and difficult birth. Peter had a malformation of his nose, a condition related to cleft lip, although only his nose was affected. In addition, I got an infection afterward which extended my hospital stay. Not having any medical insurance of our own, we were covered by the British National Health Service. The chief gynecologist resented that, and it showed in his attitude toward me. He had hoped for a private fee, but we could not afford it. Then John's boss, Lord Todd, a Nobel winner in chemistry, interceded on our behalf and treatment improved. We were grateful that we had Merete at home to help. However, at this time my Latvian friend Zinta sent us some Hungarian house guests, friends of hers, which was an additional stressor when Peter and I came home.

It was a rough start in Europe, but soon I felt very much at home in the relaxed, semirural setting of Cambridge. We biked around town. It was fun to see Nobel laureates biking to work in the rain along

Hills Road. We took weekend car trips to various destinations. Our first trip was to Ely Cathedral. On these trips we would stop for tea in the countryside and eat scones with jam and cucumber-and-cress sandwiches. After having lived in New York City for nine years, I found the leisurely pace of English life and the green English countryside, with its flocks of sheep, exceptionally healing. Many of the churches and cathedrals that we visited had medieval tombs with brass representations of their occupants. Many people used a black crayon and parchment paper to rub the brasses to obtain effigies of these ancient knights. Later I, too, became interested in rubbing the brasses. We also went to London, where I got my first really good haircut at a Vidal Sassoon salon.

In Cambridge we met Kathleen and Ian Weatherall. The Weatheralls were from New Zealand, although Kathleen was born in England. They had two little boys, Mark and Andrew. Ian was a graduate student at Emanuel College. He and John both did their research projects at the Lensfield Road Laboratories, under Lord Todd. Kathleen was a voluptuous and lively English woman with long, wavy dark-blond hair. Ian was tall, reddish blond, and exceptionally handsome.

That winter we saw the Weatheralls frequently. On weekends, the kids and the four adults would get together either at their row house on Hinton

Road or in the large kitchen of our rented house on Cavendish Avenue. There we would sip mulled wine or spiced cider while the children played on the linoleum floor with a fake brick pattern on it. Already then I was concerned about Peter's development. Ian was propping me up. "All babies will develop and walk on their own, without coaxing. You can't keep a baby from walking no more than you can stop the seasons from changing," he said with conviction. We were standing in the kitchen in front of the open fire, and I thought what an attractive man he was, with handsome Nordic features and a slightly upturned nose, so young and already so paternal. It was just a passing thought then and nothing more—not until the summer of 1991, when John and I were getting a divorce in Davis, California, and Ian showed up for a sabbatical without Kathleen.

TRAVELS

John and I both enjoyed travel. We made plans to see Spain and Morocco in the spring of 1964 together with John's friends from Austria, the Boehmes. The plan was to meet the Boehmes in Gibraltar, where their daughter Angelika was a hotel manager. She would travel with us. In preparation for the trip we learned Spanish through a BBC radio program. This course was offered at five o'clock in the evening. A study book was available in bookstores. While I cooked dinner, we listened to the voice on the BBC that taught us elementary Spanish such as "Donde est officina de tourismo?"

We were given time to repeat it as we read the sentence in the book.

We contacted the University Aunts, a group of volunteers that assisted newcomers with necessities ranging from used furniture to babysitting referrals. For child care we were referred to a farm family who lived in the area. I'm ashamed to say that we farmed out our young sons for several weeks. Another couple, Jon and Barbara Beckwith, were also going to Morocco separately from us. It was the "in thing" to do that spring. They had a son, Benjamin, who often played with our older son, Johnny. They were also leaving Benjamin on the same farm, although for a shorter period.

John and I rushed through France in our Hillman Minx. Our goal was to see Spain and Morocco; France could wait. In Spain we stayed in a parador near the Altamira Caves. An old man with a flashlight accompanied us into the prehistoric caves. There were no tours and no other visitors. Such a casual visit could not take place today. We also visited the Gaudí cathedral in Barcelona then drove through the center of Spain, through Burgos and Valladolid to Madrid. It was the week of Easter. In Valladolid men wearing conical hats and religious robes ran into a square, did some ritualistic motions, and then just as quickly departed. It seemed like religious processions were taking place in all the major cities. A procession in

Madrid impressed me in particular. People dressed in rags and chanting "Santa Maria" dragged chains through a major downtown street.

In Madrid, the conflict between Spain and Britain over Gibraltar became evident. We were traveling in a British car with British license plates. Overnight, all four of our car tires were slashed. We would have some more unpleasant experiences in Spain. On the way home, our camera would be stolen in Barcelona.

We also visited Segovia and its ancient aqueduct. We ate suckling pig in what was then a well-known restaurant at the base of the aqueduct. This is significant since this experience would later link me, many years later, to my second husband, Gerald.

On our way to Algeciras, where we would link up with our Austrian friends, we made stops in Cordova, Granada, and Seville.

We crossed the Strait of Gibraltar on a ferry together with the Boehme family and disembarked in Ceuta, Morocco. We proceeded in two cars to Fez, with the Boehmes in the lead. We lost them in a heavy rainstorm. We had made no backup plans on how or where to meet up with them, though we had talked about possibly camping in the city campground. The heavy rain made this an unlikely place to meet them. In Fez, John and I enlisted the help of the Moroccan police. John and I spent the night in a cheap hotel. The walls of the room were lined with white tile. It reminded me of a large bathroom.

The next morning, while John and I were having breakfast in a nearby café, a policeman appeared at our table. He said he had found our friends. We followed him to a home next to a campground. The Boehmes had been taken in by a hospitable family who had seen them trying to set up camp in the rain.

Fez was my first exotic experience. The marketplace teemed with storytellers, snake charmers, and merchants that sold spices and salt in bulk. Women were veiled and men wore long white robes. We visited the beautiful tiled mosques and the world's oldest university, which was also built of colorful tile.

From Fez, we proceeded over the Atlas Mountains through a barren landscape. Here and there off the road we saw a walled casbah. There was an occasional oasis with a bit of greenery, but most of the landscape was characterized by dark rock. On the south side of the Atlas Mountains, when it was time to make camp, we approached the police in Ksar es Souk, a desert outpost, about a recommendation. The chief of police declared anything outside the police compound unsafe. He invited us to set up our tents inside the compound. The negotiator on our side was Frau Boehme, who spoke passable French. The police invited us to dine with them. As a gift we offered them a tin of canned duck. They served us lamb and couscous, which we ate Arab-style on the floor, using our fingers. On the south side of the Atlas Mountains the landscape changed from black rock to sand dunes. We had reached the Sahara Desert.

After dinner, the chief of police invited us to go to a village to see Berber dancers. The older Boehmes declined, but John, Angelika, and I accepted the invitation. The police chief and one of his officers piled into our car. John drove, following their directions. All I could see in the lights of the car were sand dunes. We drove close to an hour when a building appeared. The police banged on the shuttered windows. Soon we heard whispered conversations. Then they motioned for us to come in. Inside we were greeted by women in Berber costumes. They had gold in their teeth and silver on their ankles and wrists. A pipe was passed around and we all inhaled. Then the girls started to dance. They focused their dance on John while the police chief focused his attentions on me. Angelika sat in a corner wearing an angry face. The experience was very sensual, but no sexual acts were committed. Trust and hospitality prevailed. The party never got out of hand. After a while we all piled back into the car and returned to the police compound, where we all fell asleep.

The next morning we said good-bye to our hosts and proceeded to Ouarzazate, where the Boehmes knew some people. In the tradition of true Arab hospitality, one of them, a doctor, fed and housed us, but we did not smoke or dance. We visited a hospital, where we saw families of the sick sleeping on the floor next to the patients. The doctor explained that this was the Arab way, that healing required the presence of the family.

After John and I returned from Spain, John's parents came to visit us the following summer. We traveled with them to the Scandinavian countries. We visited Norway, Sweden, and Denmark, where we stopped in to see our former au pair and her family. John and I spent two years in Cambridge, England. We traveled with both Johnny and Peter on the Continent, mostly in France, before we returned to the United States, to the Boston area, where John had a post-doctoral research position at Massachusetts General Hospital.

BOSTON AND CAMBRIDGE

We returned from England to the United States in the fall of 1965. We had left with one child and now we had two. Johnny was nearly four years old and Peter was two. I have a very fond memory from England of pushing a pram with both children in it, experiencing an exceptional moment of maternal tenderness as I watched their blond heads bob up and down as they peeked over the edge of the pram. I loved those heads so much.

In Cambridge, England, Johnny had already attended a Montessori school for six months, and I had started to teach him how to read from a kit that began with letter recognition. When we returned in

September of 1965, he was interviewed for the public kindergarten program in Brookline, Massachusetts, where we had settled. He was accepted to start kindergarten that fall.

In Brookline I used to take the children to a neighborhood park that had a sandbox. In the park I met other mothers. We sat on the ledge of the sandbox and talked. That is how I learned about the babysitting exchange. One parent would stay at home while the other parent would babysit for another family in the evening when those parents wanted to go out. A secretary kept a log of the hours. When we wanted to go out and had service hours in the bank, the secretary would send someone to babysit for us. This is how I met Patricia Staton.

Dennis and Pat had two little girls, Jenny and Laura. They were about the same age as Johnny and Peter. Soon Pat invited us over for dinner. I watched her make the salad and use the garlic press proficiently. It was the ease with which she did things that impressed me. I was also fascinated with the openness of her conversation, which in turn made me want to disclose details of my life to her. I learned that she was in psychoanalysis. We connected that evening and visited each other frequently. Pat was a psychologist who worked in Boston at an agency called Boston Educational Service and Training, which served underprivileged children in a poor neighborhood in Boston. She got me a part-time job there, which in turn later led me to a career change. Pat still lives in the Boston area and is a friend to this day.

During the time John and I lived in Brookline, several major events took place. One was the Northeast power blackout on November 9, 1965 that lasted for up to 13 hours and affected 30 million people. John rushed home to be with us. He reported how strange it was to drive through all the traffic lights that had gone dark. No explanation of the outage was ever made public.

The other event was the death of my mother. The last time I would see my mother was on Peter's birthday in November 1966. It was my mother's habit to show up for family birthdays. One day I looked down Addington Road, on which we lived, and saw my mother walking uphill toward our house. She was pulling a toy behind her. It was a wooden Snoopy on wheels for Peter's third birthday. My mother spent the weekend with us. She was still living and working in New York City in the office of the Houbigant perfume company.

We went downtown by a streetcar that ran along Commonwealth Avenue. We had coffee and cake at Schraft's. At the end of her visit my mother told me that a friend's daughter, Marija, had invited her mother, Olga, to live with her. Was she asking to live with me? My mother was sixty-one at the time and appeared in good health. I did not respond to her comment. She was then living with her boyfriend Otto, with whom she had been associated for many years. I had assumed that he would care for her. He was nine years her junior. Then my mother commented that my father had said sometime before he died that he would not want to be taken care of by me. Was she implying that I was unkind? I let that comment pass as well. I took her to the Boston train station. It was the last time I would see her.

Four months later, on March 30, a policeman rang our doorbell. We lived in an apartment on the second floor. It was midmorning. I went downstairs. I thought it had to do with a minor parking-lot accident I had had the previous week. The cop handed me a scrambled note from the cops in Brooklyn. It said my mother was in the King's County morgue. I feared my mother had been murdered, like her father had been many years ago on the farm in Latvia. My mother disdained fear and would think nothing of walking out in the middle of the night in Brooklyn to go buy a pack of cigarettes at an all-night convenience store. I called Otto. He told me my mother had died in the night just like my father had, from a heart attack. He told me then that she had worked the day before. They had gone for their customary walk in the evening. Later she had listened to the soundtrack of *Doctor Zhivago*. She was in a melancholy mood. In the morning he found her dead in her bed. My main emotion was relief that my mother had died of natural causes. Grief seeped in slowly over the years.

THE OTHER CAMBRIDGE

John worked at Massachusetts General Hospital for two years, and then got another postdoctoral position, this time at Harvard, with Bob Thach. We moved to a ground-floor apartment on Sacramento Street in Cambridge, near Harvard Square. Upstairs lived a black family named the Johnsons. They had two girls about the same age as our sons. Willard Johnson was an assistant professor at MIT. Vivian, his wife, was active in many social causes. We soon set up an intercom system between upstairs and downstairs that was turned on when the other couple went out for the evening. This way we seldom had to hire a babysitter.

The two-story rental had a backyard where the children could play. Like in Cambridge, England, we again had a pear tree in the backyard. The fence to the next door was broken, which made it easy for the children to play with the neighbor children. Jim and Barbara Walker and their two children, Julie and Jeff, lived next door. Jim was a musician and the leader of the Harvard Band. In the fall Barbara and I processed the many pears that fell from our tree. Most desserts that each of us served to guests ended up being pears flambées.

During our two years in Cambridge we partied with some of the best brains from Harvard and MIT. Finding a babysitter was not a problem. If the Johnsons were home, they would monitor our children through the intercom while John and I partied out late. In some ways the Cambridge parties were not unlike the one we attended in the Sahara Desert with the Moroccan police. Just about everyone smoked pot and there was music and dancing. Many Cambridge parties ended with a husband or a wife leaving with the spouse from another couple, like characters in an Updike novel. Some marriages survived, others disintegrated. Among those that disintegrated was Pat and Dennis's.

In hosting parties John and I experimented with different social mixes. On one occasion we only invited "interesting" people. The party was a dud because there were too many cocky men and prima donnas and not enough spectators. After strutting about for a little while everybody fled. At another time we decided to invite only "boring" people. This ended up being one of the liveliest and most successful parties we ever sponsored. Everyone participated because no one tried to dominate. Everyone was on the make, but no one broke any major social rules. We concluded that all people were interesting.

In Cambridge, Johnny attended Agassiz Elementary School, which was next door to our rented home. He became interested in ice hockey and the Boston Bruins. He developed a crush on Bobby Orr. Peter attended a nursery school for special-needs children. He learned to talk and build elaborate structures with wooden blocks. While the children were in school I spent mornings doing yoga with friends, doing crafts, or browsing the bookstores in Harvard Square. In a shop on Brattle Street I found fabric imported from Finland that I utilized to make roller shades for our front windows. In the evening, when our lights were on and the shades pulled down, from the street it looked like our windows were made of stained glass in various shades of red. I also enjoyed the Briggies on Harvard Square, where there was a soda fountain. My favorite was the mocha almond hot fudge sundae topped with whipped cream.

CALIFORNIA

On one of our western trips when we already had kids, we passed Davis, California, on Interstate 80.

"We should pull off. Check it out. There is a University of California there. I might get a job there someday," John said.

"Don't even think of it," I replied. The town was situated on a flat stretch of the interstate. Above the town, visible from the freeway, was a large water tower. This clearly was not a place where I could put down roots. I was a city girl. With the exception of Cambridge, England, and the summers spent on my grandmother's farm during the war, I had always resided in major metropolitan areas. I was not about to move to a farm town.

So we continued on the freeway to Oakland, California, where my brother lived at the time. The boys and I would spend a week with my brother and his children while John drove back east to Denver, where he was to attend a training program in neuroscience. The boys and I would fly to Denver and join him for the last week of his training. Then we would continue back to Boston, where we resided.

About a year later John got an offer from the University of California, Davis, for a tenure-track position at the newly established medical school. Other offers came from the University of California, Santa Cruz, and the University of Colorado in Boulder. The best-paying position was at Davis. He accepted it.

In the summer of 1970 we packed up our already-worn Hillman Minx with our kids and some belongings and proceeded to California by the most southern route. John was afraid that the Minx could not make it over the higher mountain passes on the more direct, northern routes. We did not want to buy a new car in Massachusetts just before we left because we would not have a dealer warranty. We would buy a car when we got to California.

The trip was uneventful until we came to the California border in some God-forsaken desert place. John, Johnny, and I cheered. Peter was confused about why we all were so happy. Later he would ask me over and over to tell him about the time we crossed the California border in the desert.

It was the first of July when we reached Needles, California. We knew we had to make it through the Mojave Desert during the night. Our Hillman would overheat. We could not risk breaking down in the desert. We checked into a motel at two in the afternoon. The boys played in the pool until supper time. We ate early, set the alarm for two in the morning, and went to sleep.

We crossed the desert in the dark without any problems. On July 2 we drove all the way from Needles to Davis. It was 110 degrees in California's Central Valley. The car had no air conditioning. When we arrived in Davis in the late afternoon, it was still 110 degrees, and this was the place where we would live.

We settled into a rented house on North Campus Way for the first year. It was a pleasant house in suburban setting. The living room opened to a garden. A white birch tree was in the center of the lawn. Birches reminded me of the birch forest next to my grandmother's farm. The tree helped me adjust to Davis.

BUILDING THE HOUSE

When we first came to California, we lived in a rental, a sabbatical house. After a year living there, we had to move to a more permanent home. I wanted to rent; John wanted to build. Because of my nomadic roots, I could not imagine living in any one place for very long. I had been uprooted when I was very young. I felt comfortable with moving on every one or two years. In fact, I needed to move on. However, John's pragmatism prevailed. We even received some money from John's parents to build the house. We picked a lot west of town, next to tomato and beet fields. We had the house custom built. We selected some of the features from our sabbatical house, such as one large living room rather than separate living and family rooms. Judging from homes that we had seen, hardly anyone used their living room. Our living room had ceiling-to-floor windows and a sliding glass door that opened up to our garden. John had wisely selected a lot that would orient the house to a southern and northern exposure rather than eastern and western. The western sun in Davis was very hot and intrusive.

The house was built in about five months. The building started in April and we moved in in September. We had no money left over to hire a landscaper, so we did our own landscaping. John graded the lot and seeded three types of grass: Kentucky bluegrass, red fescue, and New York rye. The red fescue did well in the summer, while the rye and bluegrass did better during the cooler months. We also planted eucalyptus trees in the back and orange and lemon trees in the front. We even splurged on a palm tree for the front. That was a mistake. We paid twenty-five dollars for a tiny little palm. It grew so fast that a few years later we had to pay $500 to get it removed before it fell on the house. We learned that palm trees have shallow roots. We also planted fruit trees: an apricot, a peach, and a plum tree. The apricot tree failed to thrive, but the peach and plum trees produced an abundance of fruit.

John organized a work party to build the fence. The men from his lab put in the posts and the lateral lumber that served as the base for tri-stakes. I came with a hammer and pounded in the tri-stakes. I'm ashamed to say that I did not help out on the day the posts were put in. At times I need to flee groups and lose myself in crowds, so I went off to San Francisco to shop. I pounded in the tri-stakes several days later.

We moved into the house in September. During Christmas week we decided to go camping with the kids on the beach in Baja California. It was probably my idea. I had been obsessed with seeing Mexico and we now lived within driving distance. I don't know why I was obsessed with Mexico in those days. Maybe it was the ancient religions and rituals. Maybe it was Malcolm Lowry's novel *Under the Volcano*. Camping on the beach and bringing the kids was an economic decision.

We had wonderful weather in Mexico. In each town we arrived at, it had rained the day before but the rain had moved on and driven out most tourists. We had the beach essentially to ourselves. We camped about fifty miles south of Ensenada, near a salt mine. Later we decided to visit some hot springs in the interior of Baja. We drove through the jungle and crossed many streams. When we got to the hot springs, the resort was closed. Nothing was available: no housing, not even any drinking water. We settled down for the night in an abandoned shack. In the morning John and I drank some Kahlua. It was the only food or beverage that we had in the car. Then we drove back out through the jungle, again crossing many streams.

PARIS

Twice during our marriage John and I spent his sabbaticals in Paris. The first time, in 1977, we had both Johnny and Peter with us. John had found for us an apartment that overlooked a convent-hospital garden in the thirteenth arrondissement of Paris. We could stand on the fifth-floor balcony and watch the nuns below us walk with patients in the garden. Sometimes they prayed. We felt like intruders and stepped back into our apartment.

Johnny attended a French private school nearby. For Peter we hired a tutor who took him all over Paris and taught him how to draw and paint. In addition, I found Peter an art school in the neighborhood, which he attended several times each week. While the boys were in school, I attended language classes at Alliance Française. During school vacations we traveled as a family throughout France. One of our earliest excursions was to the Loire valley and its castles. We carried the red Michelin guidebook with us. We ate dinner in Amboise after having visited the Leonardo da Vinci house and museum. At that time we did not know enough French to distinguish between *chèvre* and *cheval*. We thought we had ordered a goat-cheese dish when in fact we had ordered horse meat. Next we tried out the three-star restaurant Le Grand Vefour in Paris. The waiters recommended the selections for us. It was a grand dinner experience.

We planned our trips around Michelin-starred restaurants and architectural treasures, such as the many cathedrals, castles, and ancient abbeys of France. One spring John attended a conference in Roskoff in Brittany. We all stayed in one room at the Hotel Cheval Blanc. While John was at the meetings, Johnny, Peter, and I would visit the surrounding villages and the Calvaries that are characteristic of Brittany. Johnny was fifteen and I let him drive on the country roads and through the villages. One day all three of us sat on a bluff overlooking the Atlantic, observing the big tides that take place in the region. We also visited the famous abbey of Mont Saint Michel and spent the night there. When we arrived at Mont Saint Michel in the afternoon it was at the end of a causeway on a peninsula. In the morning it was on an island surrounded by shallow rippling water.

ON THE PATH TO POETRY

My mother was a poet. She had started writing poetry early in her life, out of necessity, after her father's murder. A high school teacher who was a Latvian poet noticed her gift for verbal expression and encouraged her to develop it. Writing poetry sustained her during the many trials of her life. Although I enjoyed reading poetry and was familiar with poems in several languages, the process of creating a poem remained a mystery to me. I never thought that I was capable of writing a poem. I believed that I was linguistically handicapped. I was fluent in several languages. I had learned German and English not because I liked languages but because I needed those languages in order to get along in the world that I was living in. I felt that I was never fully versed in any language. However, shortly before leaving for France in 1981, on an impulse, I signed up for a poetry class offered by the UC Davis Extension. The class was taught by a young graduate student named Kevin Clark. He was working on his PhD in English literature.

This class was my first venture into writing. Without Kevin, I would not be doing any creative writing today. From the very beginning, Kevin made writing poetry sound easy and fun. Our first assignment was to write a poem consisting of one stanza of four lines. Writing poetry seemed as pleasurable and as easy as putting my toe in warm water on a beach somewhere. When we turned in our assignments, Kevin had something positive to say to everyone. It was a small class. Next, he suggested topics to write about. He mentioned family members as a good place to start. I wrote about my grandmother, who had become a widow when her husband had been murdered on the farm where the family lived when my mother was a child. Kevin praised my poem and pushed me to write more. "Poetry is about overcoming," he said.

In class Kevin also read poems written by distinguished poets. He shared his poems as well. He said that hardly anyone read poetry or bought poetry books today, only other poets. He described examples of ridicule that some literary journal editors had directed toward his poems. He talked about this with a sense of amusement, not bitterness. His attitude was liberating. We learned about the frequent rejections of literary work experienced by just about any author.

In his class we learned, through demonstration and practice, how to utilize symbols, imagery, and metaphor when writing a poem. He also encouraged the use of place names when writing about a region, an idea that I took to.

When the class ended, Kevin invited us for a potluck at his home in Esparto. He had also invited some well-known local poets to the gathering so that we could find mentors and fellowship in the writing community. Kevin mentored me himself until John and I went on a sabbatical in France later that year.

At the social at his house, we also learned about regional publications and where to submit our poems. I published my first poem while still in contact with Kevin. When John and I moved to France, Kevin and I maintained occasional contact by snail mail since the Internet had not yet become widely used.

When critiquing my writing, Kevin noticed the recurrent theme of passion. "Why is passion so important?" he asked me. For this I had no answer. I learned to tone down my writing somewhat. Later I worked on how to modulate emotional openness when expressing myself in writing. This is still a work in progress.

Kevin was from what is referred to as the confessional school of poetry. He encouraged openness and emotional honesty in writing. This can, if not kept in check, lead to oversharing. Kevin was related by marriage, not by blood, to the famous fiction writer Mary Higgins Clark, who was married to his father's brother. He described some of the lavish literary parties she hosted on the East Coast.

After earning his doctorate, he found a position teaching English at Cal Poly in San Luis Obispo, where he moved up the academic ladder, eventually to full professorship. He married and raised a family. He has since published several poetry books and won numerous awards. His poems have appeared in many nationally known literary journals. In 2007 he authored a textbook entitled *The Mind's Eye: A Guide to Writing Poetry.*

MAKING THE MOST OF JULY
BIRTHDAYS

Now that I'm fast approaching eighty, some my friends are asking me if I plan to give a party. I don't like large parties and do not intend to organize one. Maybe my family will organize something and that "something" is fine with me.

As a child who was born in July, I have never had large birthday parties because we were always away from our customary surroundings at that time of year. Then, when the war started, birthday parties vanished altogether. I remember one birthday party that consisted of just my father and me. He had come from the city to my grandmother's farm during the war. He brought me a small can of sliced pineapple. The two of us ate it furtively since there was not enough to share with everyone. I think I turned six or seven that summer.

However, the birthday party I want to tell you about is my fiftieth birthday party. My husband's bio-chemistry lab group was composed for the most part of outdoor adventure lovers such as hikers, skiers, and river runners. Some of the graduate students were associated with an environmental group called Save the River. Its members could rent rafts from the organization. We rafted several local rivers, such as the American and the Klamath. Larry, a PhD student with a medical degree who worked in the lab, had applied for a permit to raft the Colorado through the Grand Canyon. It took about five years for a pri-vate party to get such a permit. As it happened, the permit was granted for July 1985, the month when I would turn fifty.

That month, thirteen of us left Davis and went off to raft the Colorado. We drove day and night, sleep-ing on picnic tables in national forests. We brought along four rented three-person rafts. No one in the group had rafted the Colorado. Larry had gone down it in a kayak, but in Utah he had found a guide who was willing to join our group. His name was Paul, and he had rafted the river several times. He was a short, middle-aged guy with long arms and a beard. To me, he looked a bit like a monkey—at all handsome. He wore old t-shirts and a pink flowered sarong wrapped around his middle like a skirt instead of trousers and wore no undergarments.

All our food, sleeping bags, and other personal belongings that had to remain dry were packed in waterproof ammunition cans. At Lee's Ferry in Arizona we attended a safety presentation given by the National Park Service, then inflated our rafts, secured the ammunition cans, and set off on the turquoise river that made its way through the red-rock country. There were thirteen people in our party and four three-person paddle rafts. There were nine men and four women on the trip. Most were members of my husband John's lab group. The plan was to raft the Colorado from Lee's Ferry in Arizona to Lake Mead, Nevada. It would take two weeks by paddle raft to travel that distance. John and I and two others planned to raft only half the distance, just one week, and disembark at the Phantom Ranch at the bottom of the Grand Canyon. At the Phantom Ranch, four other men would join the rafting party, take our places, and continue to Lake Mead.

At night we pulled our rafts onto sandy beaches among tamarisk bushes and slept in sleeping bags on the beach. I had to cook dinner for the party of thirteen on our first night out on the river. We cooked in pairs. Simon, a postdoctoral fellow from England, was my cooking partner. We made beef stroganoff using fresh presliced beef, mushrooms, green onions, sour cream, and noodles.

On most mornings the river was turquoise, but some days we woke up to a reddish-brown river. This happened when it had rained in a side canyon at night and washed the red soil into the river. Initially, we just drifted on the river and did some light paddling to keep the rafts on the course. I loved looking up at the blue sky high above the steep red cliffs and seeing birds drifting over the canyon. As the river became narrower, we started to encounter bigger rapids. We could hear the rapids from some distance before we could see them. At times the waves were high enough that they washed over our heads, leaving the raft full of water. Since the men manned the oars, my job was to bail water to the point where my back ached.

On the night of my fiftieth birthday, July 19, 1985, Antonia Bradbury, the wife of the chair of the department, was in charge of preparing dinner. I can't remember what the main course was. By then we were eating dehydrated and canned foods, but I remember a chocolate cake that she had somehow managed to make on the camp stove. John had brought along several bottles of champagne that we all shared. It was the most unforgettable birthday party I ever had.

After a few days on the river the four women—Antonia, Shannon, Lyn, and I—decided while washing our hair in the river one morning to vote on who was the sexiest man on the river. Two of us were married women. We excluded voting for our husbands out of loyalty issues. All of us agreed that Paul, the middle-aged man with his pink sarong and no underwear, was the sexiest. Barry, an MD who was about to get a PhD and who was built like a Greek god, blond and good looking, who liked to walk around naked most of the time while in camp, did not get a single vote. I think Paul's appeal was that he operated more by instinct than intellect.

The part of the Colorado River through which we traveled included several major rapids, the most challenging being the Hence Rapid. It measured a seven or eight on a ten-point scale. The night before shooting the Hence I could not sleep, in part because our camp was just up river from the Hence and we could hear its roar all night. It inspired dread. The next day while passing through the Hence I inhaled deeply, ducked my head as low as I possibly could, and then held onto the raft as tightly as I could as the water rolled over our raft and heads. Fortunately, none of our rafts capsized in the rapids.

We reached the Phantom Ranch. At the bottom of the trail, John and I and two other men left the rafting party and made room for four other men to join the group on the river. We hiked for hours up the endless red dusty switchbacks of the Bright Angel Trail. The park service had made some improvements since John and I had hiked the trail twenty-four years before. Now some drinking fountains had been added to the portion of the trail from Indian Garden up to the rim of the canyon. We broke for a late lunch at Indian Garden. When we reached the top of the South Rim at sunset I inwardly celebrated the fact that at age fifty I was still able to do what I had done when I was twenty-six: climb the five thousand feet from the bottom of the Grand Canyon to the top of the South Rim. The previous time I had carried a baby in me; now I carried a backpack full of belongings I had used on the river trip.

NEPAL

For years I used to look forward to the Sierra Club's annual listing of foreign trips. I read eagerly about trekking trips in the Himalayas and other exotic places. That was when we were still spending our summer vacations backpacking in the Sierras. Not that I was tired of the Sierras. I loved those hikes, seven-to-ten-day loop trips through the high country, carrying everything on our backs, sleeping under the stars, hiking through meadows of lupines and Indian paintbrush, just John and I, long before our marriage went sour.

We prospered. John was invited to conferences in France and Greece and other lovely places, and I went along and stayed in hotels with fabulous views. And yet, I wanted to hike in the Himalayas. However, there were no scientific conferences in that part of the world. "It doesn't make sense to go where we have to pay our own way," John said. He was a man of reason, but I had inexplicable wants.

I went back to school, got a master's degree, found a full-time job, and started to make money of my own. It was time to pursue my wants. The first vacation I planned was a Sierra Club trekking trip to Nepal. John was not enthused about it, but in the end he came along.

It started out badly. On our flight to Seattle to join the rest of the group he sat on his glasses and broke the frames. He patched them up with adhesive tape, but his mood remained grim.

There were eighteen of us gathered in front of the Thai Airways counter in Seattle for our flight to Bangkok. Our leader was Phil, a balding, gray-haired man in his early sixties. Others that stood out were Tina, a blond massage therapist from LA who wore a green velour leisure suit, and Julie, a red-haired woman from New York who kept correcting my pronunciation. When I said, "O*saka*," she said, "*O*saka"; when I mentioned *prayer* wheels, she said, "Oh, prayer *wheels*."

Sometime during our flight from Bangkok to Kathmandu we got our first views of the Himalayas.

From high up the snowcapped peaks seemed scenic and benign. They are like psychological magnets, I thought. The closer you came, the more they pulled you in, although not everyone was susceptible to their magic. The most vulnerable were those who listened to the siren songs of their own hearts.

We arrived in Kathmandu at about noon and settled in at Hotel Asia, which was located in a noisy alley. Our room faced the street. I sat on the bed and listened to the noise from the traffic below. A motorcycle or a car honked a horn every two seconds. The room was damp and a faucet dripped constantly. We rested for about one hour before our group for a tour of the city.

The city was one large exotic bazaar. Its unpaved streets were lined with small shops where merchants squatted among their wares and artisans and craftsmen toiled on sewing machines. Draped figures sat on sidewalks, temple steps, and on most available stairways. Cows and goats wandered the streets. Dogs slept on old sacks and rugs. Women wore skirts and saris; men wore Nehru-style hats. There were numerous sacrifices offered at the ubiquitous temples. Cow dung, precious in this country because it was used as fuel, was the most common offering. There was blood on the altars from chickens whose throats had been cut for more serious sacrifices. Bunches of marigolds also adorned the altars. I stood by the cosmic eye that overlooked the city. Below, a medicine man dressed in ash-colored clothes conducted a one-man ceremony in front of a home to frighten evil spirits by shaking gourds and scattering ashes.

The next day we climbed from Kathmandu Valley, at an elevation of five thousand five hundred feet, to about eight thousand three hundred feet and camped on a hillside with superb view of the Langtang Range. Just before we crawled into our tents that night, more peaks appeared out of the sea of clouds. In the distance drums beat all night to keep spirits at bay.

The next morning we were up at dawn, and after hot tea and porridge we climbed a steep hill that was followed by a very steep descent. While enjoying breathtaking views of the Himalayas I fell twice. Eventually we descended to a village where we made camp for the night. I felt very cold. The thermometer registered forty-eight degrees. A week later we would go over a pass at twelve thousand feet and walk above the clouds, and the nights would be freezing.

My marriage had chilled out as well. John and I saw each other only at meals and when we slept in the same tent at night. During the trek he was up front with the lead Sherpa and the marathon runners, but the pace of the lead pack was too fast for me. We were at an impasse. He was not slowing down for me, and I refused to run after him.

One day on the trail we met a local wedding party. The groom danced in circles, and musicians blew trumpets at us and asked for dollars. The bride was dressed in red from head to toe.

Hiking in Nepal was like walking from Tibet to India. The villages were inhabited by pure ethnic groups, either Sherpas or Hindus. In the high country lived the Sherpas, in the low lands the Hindus. There were wide differences in customs between the two groups. The Sherpas were aloof and kept their distance. The Hindus liked close contact. The small Hindu children were very inquisitive. A small boy touched my sleeping bag, and a little girl fingered my bracelet.

Eventually we all had had enough of Nepal. None of us had taken a bath or shower since leaving Kathmandu. We were tired of tasting iodine in our drinking water and eating curry at night. On our last day our group hiked to a place where we could get a view of Mount Everest, then headed home.

Years later, after my divorce from John, and after a number of years on my own, I met a man, fell in love, and married him on Valentine's Day. Because it was Valentine's Day, I decided to wear a red dress and shoes. After I had finished dressing, I looked in the mirror and experienced a moment of recognition. We had met before, but where? Then I remembered the bride dressed in red I had met on the trail in Nepal.

ON MY OWN

On the cusp of 1990–91, John and I took a trip to India with the Haverford College Alumni Association from John's alma mater. We did not know it yet, but it was to be our last big trip as a couple. We flew on Singapore Airlines, survived a layover in the Taipei airport, and ended in Singapore up for New Year's Eve. We spent the evening walking with the people of Singapore. Everyone seemed to be in the street, men, women, and children, all wearing glow rings. We spent two days exploring the city. Rafters Hotel was being remodeled so we could not have a drink there, but we caught a wonderful thunderstorm in the botanical gardens. We enjoyed delicious giant prawns from a street vendor in Newton Circle.

We arrived in Delhi late at night, ahead of the rest of the party. Upon arrival, a member of the hotel staff offered us a sweet exotic fruit drink in our room. In the morning we left the hotel to explore the city. We noticed what we thought were dog feces in front of the hotel. However, later we learned that they were human feces deposited by the shantytown inhabitants. The shantytown was just around the corner from our luxury hotel. The hotel was in New Delhi. New Delhi had broad avenues like a European city. Old Delhi had narrow streets and alleys and exotic markets. We took a taxi to the marketplace in Old Delhi. Veiled women did their shopping in the old town market. Sheep skulls were piled up in a pyramid and animal carcasses were displayed by butchers. Spice merchants and the aromas of their wares dominated the scene. An old woman dressed in black and carrying a clump of branches come toward me and then hit my forehead with the branches. Maybe this was an omen that I failed to grasp at the time.

After touring Delhi with the group, including seeing the world's dirtiest toilet next to the Red Fort, we departed by chartered bus to Agra, where we visited the Taj Mahal in the early morning. From there we traveled to the desert of Rajasthan, where camels and people pulled burdens instead of horses. Before returning to Delhi we visited Jaipur and saw the Amber Fort.

The Gulf War started while we were in India. We watched it all on CNN. At the same time, the Soviet Union was breaking apart. CNN showed us images of people fighting in Latvia and Lithuania. Suddenly, the suppressed fears from World War II emerged full blown in my mind. I became fearful. After visiting the northern cities of India we were scheduled to visit predominantly Muslim parts of India such as Hyderabad. In the early 1960s we had traveled to Morocco, a predominantly Muslim country. In Morocco, at a desert outpost, we had partied and smoked a pipe with a police chief named Mahmed. Fear had not entered my mind. Now, in India, in January 1991, I wanted to get out of the tour, abort the trip, fly back to the safety of the United States. As it turned out, my intuition was not entirely off. The luxury hotel Taj Mahal, located in the Mumbai harbor and where we were staying, would be attacked by terrorists from the sea some ten years later, an event that was featured in international news.

Back in the States our relationship deteriorated. John worked long hours in the lab while I went on shopping sprees in the evenings. Then, on April 30, 1991, our nearly thirty-two-year marriage fell apart in our kitchen. I had prepared a dinner with a dessert. I don't remember what the main course was, but the dessert was to be strawberries with whipped cream.

John launched a verbal attack. "Why don't you have any friends?" It was hurtful. As an immigrant, I have at times felt like an outsider, and this comment struck a sensitive chord. I worked out of town, and my friends were my coworkers. I was holding a dish of whipped cream in one hand and another dish of strawberries in the other.

"Because...because..." I responded. Then I decided not to justify myself. Instead, I dropped the whipped cream on the floor and then the strawberries. Then John charged, kicked me in the back, and ran out the front door.

My main reason for wanting to break free from my marriage was John's compulsive need to entertain. As a professor he could come in late to work to do his research since his teaching load was minimal, about ten hours per academic year. His lab was in Davis, not at the Sacramento Medical Center. He could bike to work. By contrast, I commuted close to one hour each way to work and had to sign in at 8:00 a.m. He was his own boss while I had a program director above me. I felt constantly pressured by John to entertain visiting foreign academics. Much of their conversation was centered on the politics of science and whose projects were getting funded and who failed to get a grant. Much to his credit, John never failed to get a research grant. Research grants from the National Institutes of Health and other funding organizations like the American Cancer Society brought in money to the UC Davis Medical School. However, this talent also made him arrogant and demanding. He had been a long-distance runner in college; now he was an unrelenting social director. Due to time spent commuting, work pressures and lack of sleep, I could not keep up with his pace, as I had not been able to in Nepal. In addition, I had my own career and interests that required time.

SUMMER OF 1991

The year 1991 was to become my summer of love. I never expected it. John and I were ending a marriage of almost thirty-two years, but we still lived under the same roof. John was going to France for meetings, and we had made plans to travel together in Europe afterward. I had saved up vacation time so I could do that. As his departure approached, he told me I was still welcome to come along. I did not say yes or no. Instead I called my brother. He was making plans that summer to drive to the top of the North American continent, as far as the roads could take him, to an Inuit village called Inuvik. I asked him if I could join him. He said yes. Then I told John that I planned to use my vacation time to go north with my brother rather than to with him to France. This choice accelerated the end of our marriage.

In mid-June I flew to Vancouver, where my brother met me with his new white truck. We drove north for days on end, through British Columbia, along snow-capped mountains to the west, camping along the way, eating rice and beans cooked on a camp stove in the evening, and splurging on oatmeal-with-bacon breakfasts in the midmorning at restaurants along the way. We drove on the Alaska-Canada highway, known as Al-Can for short, until we came to the Yukon, where the paved road ended, and then proceeded on a gravel road, the Dempster, to the Northwest Territories, the big sky opening before us. We crossed the Mackenzie River on a raft, leaving all our troubles behind. We read poems by Robert Service and visited Jack London's cabin in the Yukon. My brother was divorced at the time, teaching at a community college in Portland, and had the summer off.

We reached Inuvik in mid-July, and it was snowing. We finally splurged on a motel. On the way home we stopped in Tok, Alaska, and spent a night in Skagway before returning home. One morning during our return, we looked back and saw an enormous moose standing on the road, silhouetted against the rising sun.

During the breakup I had reached out to my brother. Our parents were no longer living. Other than my two sons my brother was my closest relative. He was also a veteran of marital wars. On our road trip to the Northwest Territories, he did all the planning, cooking, and driving. In the evenings he wrote in his journal. I did not document this trip. I have a general memory of this trip as described above. However, my brother's account provides significant details about this distant region of Canada where very few people venture. The following is an excerpt from my brother's memoir based on his diary of our joint venture into this remote far northern region of Canada:

In the summer of 1991 I had a plan to drive to Inuvik on the Dempster Highway, which would be at that time how far north one could drive on a public road in North America. On the way back I wanted to drive on the Cassiar Highway, which is to the west of the Alaska Highway. The children had grown up, I was single again, and then my sister asked if she could come along. "Why not?" I answered. I had a different vehicle, a 1991 Chevrolet S-10 pickup truck. My sister had just gotten divorced, so I guess her coming along was a form of post-divorce travel therapy. As she lived in California and I in Oregon, we agreed to meet in Delta, BC, near the Vancouver airport. I drove up from Portland, and she arrived that evening by airplane.

The next day we headed north. It was mid-June. Our plan was to camp and then every third or fourth day check into a motel in order to take a shower and enjoy some of the other benefits of civilization, and that is pretty much how the trip went.

In Dawson City we visited the restored cabin of Robert Service, the famous bard of Yukon and the North. Then we proceeded to the Dempster Highway. This highway is like what the Alaska Highway used to be, a gravel road. It has in places panoramic views of awesome scope, where it rides on the top of a mountain ridge and provides views of valleys and other mountains in the distance. One should fill up before starting, as the next gas station is at Eagle Plains 230 miles north. Eagle Plains had a restaurant, a hotel, and a campground that was open all year. Time to fill up again, and from here one should be able to make it to Inuvik, another 235 miles away. Twenty-two miles further up the road was the Arctic Circle. There was a place to pull off the highway and meet the official greeter of the Arctic Circle, in all his finery. Dick North was the gentleman pulling this duty, and my sister also bought his book about the Mad Trapper of Rat River.

On the way to Inuvik two rivers must be crossed. At both, the Peel River and the Mackenzie, there are free ferries, which operate in the ice-free season. The total length of the Dempster Highway is 465 miles[;] thus Eagle Plains is pretty much the midpoint.

Inuvik is where the road ends. It is the largest Canadian community north of the Arctic Circle. It is a new town. Its construction began in 1955 and was completed in 1961. It is located on a flat wooded plateau on the east channel of the Mackenzie River, about [sixty] miles south of the Beaufort Sea. All the buildings sit on stilts[,] and the water and plumbing connections are also above ground[,] connecting between buildings and insulated and presumably heated so that they do not freeze during the long and cold winter. It is a weird sight. We were there during the time of the midnight sun, but the temperatures were in the forties Fahrenheit, and I remember when we crossed the mountain pass where the Yukon and Northwest Territories meet it was snowing and the snow was sticking to the road.

We walked around town, visited the Igloo Church (built in the round shape of an igloo), and checked out the local bookstore and supermarket, where a wide variety of goods were available. We spent one night in a motel in Inuvik and then headed back.

From Dawson City we took the ferry across the Yukon River and proceeded into Alaska on the Top of the Word Highway. This is one of the most scenic drives in the world. The highway runs on top of a ridge with panoramic views on both sides. The green of the forests [and] the clearings full of blooming fireweed added a variety of colors to the scene. Later on —it might have been the next day — we enjoyed a salmon feed in Tok, and camped in a campground with hot showers. Someplace near here there had been a forest fire in one of the prior years. We walked through a devastated but recovering area. Our drive took us back into Yukon and into Alaska again and on to Skagway where to our surprise a we saw a cruise ship docked in the harbor.

When I got home, John had moved to an apartment, leaving behind, mixed among music sheets left on the piano, a copy of *People* with a label addressed to a Panda Chen. I knew then that our marriage was over. I had planned for such eventualities and had scheduled activities for the rest of the summer. First, I attended a writing workshop in Napa. When I returned from the workshop I signed up for a Sierra Club hike on Angel Island. Then, on the evening before the hike, I received a phone call from Ian, whom I had met many years ago in Cambridge, England, and had not seen for many years. He said he was in Davis on a sabbatical and asked if I would see him. I invited him to join me on the hike to Angel Island in the morning, which he did. We had dinner that evening in the garden at my house, followed by many nights of dinner, drinks, and togetherness. In a summer of the extreme North, love had blown in from the South Island of New Zealand.

Ian returned to New Zealand in the winter of 1991. After the door closed behind him for the last time, I threw myself on the couch and cried "Sofija," my grandmother's name. She was the one who had lost everything, first her husband when he was murdered, in 1919, and again when we left her behind on the farm alone, during the World War II, in 1944. Like her, I was in my life alone. I drew strength from my grandmother's ancestral spirit and from Robert Frost's poem "Bereft," with which I was already familiar: "I was in the house alone...I was in my life alone..." I would never see Ian again. He would die in Queensland, Australia, in the summer of 2005.

ROBERT

Facebook sent me a message reminding me of Rob's birthday, October 21. I should have updated my friends list. Rob had died earlier in the year. He was seventy-eight.

About a decade ago there would have been a party, a pig roast in his backyard, lots of people, lots of drinks. Then, during this past decade, he slowly withdrew. He interacted with me mostly by phone, sometimes calling several times a day. He also sent me a Christmas gift each year that was delivered by FedEx, even though he lived around the corner from me. During the last few years of his life he sent me amaryllis bulbs in pots. With careful watering, a month or two later they would burst forth into beautiful red blossoms. There were also some late-night parties at his house with his drinking buddies, attended mostly by Russians and his Russian girlfriend Olga. Then Olga distanced herself from Rob. She was his last girlfriend.

Rob was an exceptionally intelligent man. Born in Utica, New York, he received his bachelor's degree in chemistry from Haverford College in Pennsylvania in 1956. He and John met at Haverford and roomed together during their second year in college. Rob received his PhD from Rockefeller University in 1962. After completing postdoctoral work at the Medical Research Center in Cambridge, England, he worked at the University of Geneva in Switzerland for six years in the field of protein synthesis. He was hired as assistant professor at UC Davis in 1970 and in due time earned tenure and became a full professor.

Our lives intertwined more than either of us had expected. Rob knew me longer than most of my family members. My brother has been in my life the longest. John and Rob had known me equally long until Rob died in 2012. I met John and Rob on the same day. We lived parallel lives in New York, in Cambridge, England, and in Davis. While still young, John, Rob, a girlfriend of Rob's, and I would go on camping trips together. Our first joint camping trip was to a beach on Long Island. John and I shared a tent and so did Rob and Inge, the Estonian girl who was with me when Rob and John and I met at the Rockefeller Christmas party. Once, John and I went to Lake George with Rob and his eventual wife, Sheila, for canoeing and camping. Another time, shortly before John and I got married, we went on a camping trip to Mount Marcy in the Adirondacks.

After John and I split up in 1991, and Ian returned to his life in New Zealand, Rob remained my closest male friend locally. We lived around the corner from each another. We had dinners together, mostly at his place, and occasionally went out to dinner or went to a movie. Once, after we had had a good dinner at his house and Rob had had one too many drinks, he took my hand and said, "You could eat like this every night." He implied we could live together, negotiate our wants and needs, including sex, and have as little or as much as we might want. I did not know how to respond, and said little. Rob drank too much, and I had met Jerry, who would become my future husband. My relationship with Rob remained platonic to the end.

When I first met Rob at the Rockefeller Christmas party in 1958, it never crossed my mind that I would be the one who would send him to the hospital for the last time on the day he died, February 29, 2012. Rob's last days were as follows. I received a call from his son, Ashley, on Monday night, February 27, saying that Rob was not answering his phone. Jerry and I went over and knocked on his door. He yelled that he could not come to the door but that it was open. His mail was still outside, and inside there were stacks and stacks of papers that looked like unopened mail. He was in his kitchen sipping something from a small glass and watching TV. He told us he had been in the hospital. The grocery store where he shopped had notified the authorities when he had not showed up for his usual shopping. He had not gone there because several days ago he had had a fall and was in pain. The authorities came to his house, confiscated his dog, and sent him to the hospital. He had left the hospital against medical advice on the day we were talking. I told him about Ashley's call. I was not sure if Rob had paid his bills lately or if his phone was working. His cell phone battery had died. He told me where the charger was. I brought it to him. I told him that he should call Ashley from the cell. He said he would. Then he went off to bed. Soon after we left Rob's house he called me to thank for checking up on him. He said Ashley might come out in a few days.

Jerry and I stopped by the next day. Rob was in bed. He was concerned that his dog would be put to sleep by the authorities. A former co-worker of his, Joachim, was trying to find a vet who could treat Rob's dog. The dog had cancer. Rob seemed coherent and in touch with reality. We brought him a ham-and-cheese croissant for lunch and then we left.

We stopped by again the following day. Rob was still in bed. The croissant we had brought the day before was still at his bedside. He had had an accident. He was very emotional and said that Joachim could not find a vet who could treat his dog and had had the dog put to sleep and cremated. There was an empty Korbel champagne bottle at his bedside. I asked if Joachim was coming back.

"No," Rob said.

Jerry and I were at a loss what to do. We went home and decided to call 911. We went back to Rob's house and met with the medics, who remembered being there a few days ago. I told Rob that the medics had arrived, that we were going to send him back to the hospital to get him back on his feet. The last time I saw Rob, he was strapped on a gurney about to be put in the ambulance. We did not follow him to the hospital. Somehow I thought Rob was invincible. He had complained about his health for many years, in all of his phone conversations. I thought that hypochondriacs were immortal. I thought that what Rob needed was hydration by IV, that he would return home and Ashley would come and make the necessary support arrangements. Instead, Rob died at the Sutter Davis hospital that evening.

Joachim called me and said that he had brought the champagne that was at Rob's bedside, that the two of them had drank it to ease the pain of losing the dog. Joachim insisted that Rob had wanted to die, and yet I noticed that Rob had just planted a small red bud that was in bloom and that there was a newly refilled bottle of medication on the kitchen table.

WINDING DOWN

Today I went to see Cap. He is a substitute for Peggy, a psychotherapist that I had seen on and off during my years in Davis. But he has more to offer. He has a prescription pad. I need pills to boost my mood; I need pills for sleep.

His office is very pleasing. It contains three leather chairs, a desk, a couch, and an oriental carpet on the floor. There are diplomas on the wall and a pleasing view of a tree-covered street. No green lamp to light my way, but I see him in the daytime. His favorite dog, Rory, lies on the carpet as I enter. The dog knows me and does not bark.

What is remarkable about Cap is that he has come back from the dead. About ten years ago he dropped dead while jogging with some friends. One of them had a cell phone. They were able to summon the medics quickly. Cap was resuscitated. Now he is back practicing medicine. Psychiatry is his field.

I talk about my mood, my sleep patterns, my aches and pains. Today he says, "If you are drinking, keep drinking; if you are not drinking, start drinking." In other words, I don't have much time and I should do whatever I please.

How do I want to spend my time? What matters to me the most? Travel used to be a pick-me-up. Now it tires me out. I don't want to die far from home. The other night I woke up with a severe pain on my left side. I thought it might be a heart attack. We were planning to go to Oregon in a few days to meet my son John and my brother. I knew I would have to call off the trip. I wondered if I should wake Jerry and ask him to take me to the emergency room, but I did not want to lie on a cot with light shining in my eyes. I wanted the comfort of sleep or oblivion. So I turned over on my stomach and somehow managed to go back to sleep. In the morning I was fine. We proceeded with the trip to Oregon.

In Oregon it was not me who needed emergency services. It was my friend Zinta. She was sipping a margarita when she slipped from the stool and passed out on the floor. She too declined emergency services.

Cap has shown me that you can come back from the dead, although I'm not sure that I would want to. Just recently he and Helen went to New Zealand, where they rented a car and toured the country on their own. More recently, they went to Uganda and climbed to seven thousand feet to see the silverback gorillas. He said they came very close to a pair. The male tried to shelter the female.

"He was afraid you would try to steal her from him," I said.

Later I drove to Woodland to a nursery to buy some winter-blooming flowers for the flower- bed outside the kitchen window. I bought some pink snapdragons and a six- pack of mixed pansies and planted them. I look forward to seeing them bloom.

DIVORCE AND REMARRIAGE

My brother, Neil, and I found new loves in our retirement years. John and I divorced in 1992. At that time I was working for the State of California as a government program analyst in Sacramento. About five years earlier I had returned to school and earned a master's degree in social work. I was no longer a chemist. I was now a bureaucrat writing documents for the State of California. In the local singles scene I met a former neighbor named Gerald Gibbons. Gerald had retired from the air force, where he had reached the rank of colonel. He, too, had recently divorced. We had a lot in common. We had both been married years to other people for thirty-two. While in the air force, Gerald had lived in England and Spain. We had both eaten suckling pig with our former spouses at the same restaurant in Segovia, Spain, under the ancient aqueduct.

After dating for several years, Jerry and I married on Valentine's Day, 1998. My brother had married for the third time the previous year. He had married a former co-worker named Lynn, a retired nursing instructor he had met at Mount Hood Community College. All four of us were financially secure, having worked in public sector jobs. For a number of years the four of us traveled together to distant lands.

ASSISTED LIVING

A few summers ago Jerry and I went on a cruise with Neil and Lynn on the St. Lawrence River from Montreal to Boston. Neil and Lynn have cruised the world with the Holland America Line many times. With their help we were able to obtain relatively comfortable quarters next door to one another on a ship called the *Maasdam*. It was a mid-sized cruise ship.

On a cruise ship everything is provided: meals, clean rooms, and entertainment. In other words, it is a form of assisted living. We had a small room on one of the lower decks. It was a basic room with two twin beds and a full window. Neil and Lynn had an identical room next to ours. The rooms had a public address system, and shortly after boarding we were summoned to the deck to participate in a safety drill. After the drill we had time to unpack and relax. Later we watched the ship set sail from the Crow's Nest, a bar on the twelfth floor of the ship. As Montreal receded in the distance, we went down to dinner. That evening we ate at a table for four in an elegant dining room. We were to eat at the same table at 6:00 p.m. every evening.

That evening, tired from the boarding experience and the general excitement, we turned in early. We were soundly asleep when, in the middle of the night, there was a loud rumble in the public address system. I glanced at the clock. It was midnight. Soon we went back to sleep and then were awoken again by the same type of noise. The time was 2:00 a.m. Now I was fully awake and angry, my mind unsettled. Are we going to be trapped in a cabin for seven nights with a public address system that was designed to drive people crazy? At 7:00 a.m. I called the front desk to report the disturbance. I was told that a team of engineers was working on identifying the problem. At breakfast I talked to my brother. Yes, he had heard the noise in the public address system but it didn't bother him. He told me if the situation upset me then it was my problem. My brother does not tolerate complaints. One of his favorite pronouncements is "Life is tough and then you die." I fully expected him to declare that life is tough and then you die, but to his credit he had the grace to turn and walk away.

On and off during the day the public address system cleared its throat. While the engineers worked on it, we tried to enjoy the assisted-living part of the cruise. Next to the substantial swimming pool there was a cafeteria that was open twenty-four/seven. There were delicious hamburgers with freshly sliced onions and tomatoes, roast turkey, beef, seafood salads, Mexican food, Italian food, Asian food, and sandwich meats. However, the best were the desserts: puddings, cookies, hot fudge sundaes, cakes, tarts, and fruit cobblers. My favorite was the bread pudding, for which I returned time and again. No grocery shopping, no cooking, no dishes to wash, no meals to plan, no need to make up the bed: it's quite a life.

In the evening, after dinner, we went to the show or enjoyed drinks together in the music room, where a trio of young Russians played classical music. At 11:00 p.m. there was chocolate tasting but I never lasted that long.

Despite the imperfect start, the rest of the trip was delightful. The public address system remained quiet at night, the food was perfect, and the service was impeccable. Each day we docked in a different town or city: Quebec, Charlottetown, Sydney, Halifax, Bar Harbor, and Boston. In each town a tour bus took us to some quaint destination such as the house of *Anne of Green Gables*, a fantasy house (since Anne never lived in it) where we could walk in the surrounding woods among blue forget-me-nots.

We ended the trip with a three-day stay in Boston. What was the best part of the trip? Despite the rocky start, it was the company of my brother that made the trip memorable for me. My brother was my constant companion during my early years. As children we explored the forests and meadows on our grandmother's farm. Later, as refugees, we explored various towns in Germany. During World War II and the years following the war, Germany was overrun by refugees from Eastern Europe. Young Germans referred to us as *Ferfluchte Auslander*. It translates roughly to "damn foreigners." Together we had experienced life-threatening attacks during the war. In those years we had moved from town to town, sleeping in cheap hotels, train stations, and air-raid shelters, and we were later settled in DP camps. Once, when my brother and I were gathering wild berries in a forest near Bayreuth, we were chased by German youths with dogs.

About twenty years ago, when both Neil and I were between marriages, we traveled together to places such as Alaska, Finland, and Latvia, often camping or staying at inexpensive hotels or with relatives in Latvia. Now I was grateful that we had survived and had remained travel companions into old age, enjoying assisted living together on a cruise ship.

So there, Brother: life is tough, but you get to cruise before you die.

Once, a long, long time ago, in another country, in another century, on another continent, our family of four—my father, mother, brother, and myself—had crossed a broad boulevard in Riga, Latvia, when I was still a small child, the youngest in the family. My brother and I both wanted to hold our father's hands, and my mother lamented that no one wanted to hold hers. Oh, what I would give now to hold her hand for even a moment.

I am the only person left of the four family members who crossed the street on that sunny afternoon in Riga. Our parents died many years ago, and Neil died on December 21, 2016, in Portland, Oregon. I find myself alone and empty-handed. Yes, I have found other hands to hold in my lifetime, the hands of lovers, children, relatives, and friends, and still have loving hands within reach: my grown children's hands, the hands of my husband, current family members, and friends.

But nothing remains in our hands forever. Everything we keep slowly slides through them. Fate links them together for greetings and farewells.

48840410R00112

Made in the USA
San Bernardino, CA
07 May 2017